Eartha & Kitt

Eartha
& Kitt

A Daughter's Love Story
in Black & White

KITT SHAPIRO
and Patricia Weiss Levy

PEGASUS BOOKS
NEW YORK LONDON

EARTHA & KITT

Pegasus Books, Ltd.
148 West 37th Street, 13th Floor
New York, NY 10018

First Pegasus Books cloth edition May 2021

Interior design by Sheryl P. Kober

All interior images courtesy of the Archives of Kitt Shapiro.

Images at the bottom of image insert page 4, and on page 5, taken by Lennart Nilsson.

Images from Kittsville Studio taken by Howard Morehead.

ISBN: 978-1-64313-754-4

10 9 8 7 6 5 4 3 2 1

Printed in the United States of America
Distributed by Simon & Schuster
www.pegasusbooks.com

Mom, you were right, you can never love
a child too much. Thank you.
—K.S.

To Aidan and Allegra, the subjects of
my own mother-child love story.
—P.W.L.

CHAPTER 1

The Most Exciting Woman in the World

I'm not black and I'm not white
and I'm not pink and I'm not green.

My mother may have been known as a consummate talent, coy sex kitten, and courageous trailblazer who helped break down racial barriers, but she began her long, illustrious life in a distinctly different way. As she would be the first to tell you, she was "just a poor cotton picker from the South." And no matter how far she got in life—and considering that she was world-famous by the time she was 23, and was still headlining when she was 81, I'd say that she went pretty far—on some level she still always felt like "just a poor cotton picker from the South."

She starred in many Broadway shows, from *New Faces of 1952* and *Timbuktu!* to *The Wild Party* and *Nine*, and performed her consistently sold-out one-woman show in Las Vegas, London, New York, Paris, and other major cities throughout the world. She made dozens of movies, from *Anna Lucasta* and *St. Louis Blues* to *Boomerang* and *The Emperor's New Groove*; recorded 40 albums, both studio and live; was nominated for three Tony Awards, three Emmys, and two Grammys, several of which she won; and wrote three autobiographies, including one called *I'm Still Here*, for no matter what befell her in life—and an awful lot of tough stuff invariably did—she would always pick herself up again and still be *there*.

She spoke four languages, sang in seven, and had a unique, unforgettable sound—a voice for the ages that was mysteriously unidentifiable in geographic origin, yet unmistakably hers. And who hasn't heard her many classic hit songs, including "C'est Si Bon" and "Santa Baby," the best-selling Christmas song of 1953 and still an evergreen staple of the holiday season?

Her music remains as popular and relevant as ever, as evidenced by the soundtracks of the widely acclaimed HBO superhero series *Watchmen*, starring Regina King, and the hit Netflix series *Emily in Paris*, starring Lily Collins. Never mind that she may be best known by many today for playing her iconic role as Catwoman, the Caped Crusader's feline adversary, on the 1960s TV series *Batman*.

Yet she was far more than just a celebrity who commanded both stage and screen. Along with being an outspoken civil rights activist who avidly supported Dr. Martin Luther King Jr., she served as a tireless social advocate on behalf of historically-underserved youth, gay rights, women's rights, and countless other causes. Then there was that infamous incident at the White House. The one when she stood up to the First Lady, Lady Bird Johnson, at a luncheon in 1968, daring to voice her opposition to the Vietnam War, a defiant move, unheard of by celebrities in those times, which caused the CIA to compile a defamatory dossier on her, characterizing her as a "sadistic sex nymphomaniac." That controversial episode nearly derailed her career.

Orson Welles once pronounced her "the most exciting woman in the world." Yet the one achievement she was the proudest of was not any of those things.

What she prided herself on most by far was having brought a mutt into this world.

And when I say "mutt," I mean me.

Despite the many famous men to whom my mother was linked romantically, all before I was born, there could be no question who the one true love of her life was.

Revlon founder Charles Revson? Entertainer Sammy Davis Jr.? Actor James Dean? New York banking heir John Barry Ryan III? MGM Studios scion Arthur Loew? No, no, no, no, no.

It was her one and only child. Her daughter, Kitt.

That would also be me.

She named me Kitt because she wanted to make sure that her name would be carried on. Regardless of whether I turned out to be a boy or a girl—and until I popped out on that Sunday afternoon in November of 1961, she didn't know which—that's who I was going to be.

"I'm Eartha, and this is Kitt," she would declare to almost everyone we ever met. She would make that comment as though I completed her. And in many ways, I did.

Complete her, I mean. And vice versa. We were a really good fit for each other.

I got it. Got *her*, that is—who she was, and who and what she needed me to be. Those were things that, instinctively, I always understood. She needed me to care for her. Needed me to be *there* for her. Needed me to give her the roots that she never had.

Having been given away by her young single mother and never having known who her father was, who could really blame her?

When I was a little girl, she would put me to bed herself almost every single night, and we would read books together. One of my favorites was *Are You My Mother?* But for me that question was never in doubt. Never mind the notable differences in our appearance. She was mine, and I was hers. As if we were meant to be. I would often say to her, "I picked you! God had me pick *you* for my mommy." How funny that I remember thinking that I had intentionally chosen her. Yet now, looking back, I sometimes describe it as believing that God, or some sort of higher power, had decided, "You would be a really good fit with her."

I look back now on our life together, and it really is a love story. There are people who believe that there is only one person put on this earth for them, and that all they need to do is find that person. Well, I never needed to go find my person. I had already found her the moment that I was born. At least in terms of being a mother and daughter, we came about as close as any two people conceivably could to being a perfect match.

No, I'm not saying that she was a perfect mother. That would be a stretch for anyone. And honestly, how could she have been? Never really having been mothered herself, she didn't have any real role models when it came to parenting. She followed her gut and her instincts and sometimes had to make it up as she went along.

But I have no doubt that I was a really good fit for her as a daughter. For one thing—and I think that this really helped—I never aspired to become an entertainer myself. I didn't have any real desire to have my own spotlight. I already had a spotlight. My mother, as famous as she was herself, always put the spotlight on me.

Or maybe it's that my mother *was* the spotlight on me. As a little girl, isn't that all that you really want—for your parent to pay attention to you and think that you're the greatest thing ever? Well, my mother thought I was the greatest thing ever. She didn't do it to the point at which she indulged me, though. I was never, ever spoiled. On the contrary, she was strict as a mom, and always insisted that I have good manners and be well-behaved. She had a sense of command about her that made you fall in line. Everyone around her always did. Anything else wasn't going to be tolerated, so you really had no choice. What's interesting is that she wasn't a person who ever yelled or screamed. She never threw fits in any form or fashion. It was more that she had this regal presence. She had an aura, an innate energy about her, that people, animals, and virtually all living things picked up on. It made you *want* to behave.

My mother may have been known as an international sex symbol—an image that she carefully cultivated to her dying day—but here's the first big secret that I'll share with you: Behind the scenes, my mother was far from risqué, in the sense of being lewd or the least bit crude. She was actually quite proper. She shunned profanity. Shied away from almost any mention of sex. You might even say she was a prude.

She was also very much a stickler for manners. She demanded good behavior. Especially from me. She expected me to act like a lady. That may have just been a product of the times in which we lived, but if you were female, she believed that you had to be ladylike. That didn't mean that you weren't strong and independent, as she decidedly was herself. You just had to behave like a lady. One thing that ladies don't do, apparently, is chew gum in public. That was absolutely forbidden in front of my mother.

Many things were forbidden by my mother. I'm not talking about crazy things like "no wire hangers," as Joan Crawford's daughter Christina divulged in her tell-all book *Mommie Dearest*. I mean any kind of poor behavior. Like whining. Or talking too much. Or talking too loudly. Or cursing. Or being late.

Tolerant, she was not.

She wasn't a difficult person per se. But she could be very demanding.

And even though she had the means and maybe the desire to spoil me, she never did. My manners were impeccable. In fact, the entire staff at the Plaza Hotel (where we often stayed when my mother performed in New York City in the 1960s) knew who I was. They called me "the good Eloise," as opposed to the wayward six-year-old in the classic book series. I was the little girl who never got into trouble. The one who waited patiently in her mother's dressing room while her mother was onstage. An only child who learned to entertain herself while her mother was busy entertaining the rest of the world.

Yes, I was a good Kitt to her Eartha. And she was the ultimate Eartha to my Kitt. We were a team. Inseparable. From the first day of my life to the very last day of hers.

As an adult, that meant that I served not only as her manager, but also sometimes her spokesperson, even in the most mundane situations. She had one of the world's most recognizable voices, and yet I often served as her voice. For there's another thing that might surprise you. Despite my mother's brazen public image and her sensual, coquettish stage persona, she was extremely shy. At least she often felt that way when she was meeting someone for the first time, or walking into a room full of strangers. Me, on the other hand? People have called me many things over the years. Given the self-confidence that was instilled in me, shy is not one of them. I had no trouble introducing her to others or speaking up on her behalf.

There are people who may even think that I'm a little too loud. My mother's longtime musical director, Daryl Waters, for one. He worked with her for at least thirty years. I once remarked to him that I was just a delicate flower, and he looked at me and said, "Sweetheart, you're a cactus if I ever met one."

And I said, "Cacti have flowers as well, and they take no crap from the outside, so I take that as a compliment."

No doubt this book will appeal to my mother's many fans—including her hundreds of thousands of followers on Facebook—who still abound across all generations over a decade after her death. I hope it will also find an audience among those seeking strong female role models (for my mother unquestionably was one of the strongest you will ever find). It should speak as well to all women, and men as well, who love their mothers, may have lost their mothers, or who yearn to have a person in their lives who filled that role. And it has the added dimension of being an interracial mother-daughter love story, between a pair who looked very different on the surface, even if my mother defied anyone to define what either of our racial identities was.

She herself penned three autobiographies—*Thursday's Child* in 1956, *Alone with Me* in 1976, and *I'm Still Here: Confessions of a Sex Kitten* in 1989—plus a memoir in 2001 called *Rejuvenate (It's Never Too Late)*. Yet the truth is that I can offer a very different perspective. A unique perspective. And in many ways, a truer, or at least more objective, one. For I was the one person on the planet who truly knew her best.

Besides, the tale that I have to tell you is not the story of my mother's life. It is, rather, the story of my amazing life *with* my mother. The mother I loved. The mother I miss every day. The mother whom millions admired, but only I truly knew.

I knew what it was like for her when she was blacklisted during the Vietnam War and was unable to perform almost anywhere in her own country for nearly ten years.

I knew what it was like for her to walk me down the aisle at my wedding—not once, but twice—feeling like she was losing her only daughter, the one that she doted and depended on, rather than gaining a son.

I knew just what she meant when she said, "I don't have to be wealthy to be rich." Or, "The only thing I can sell and still own is my talent."

Or, "Sometimes it's good to fall down to see who will pick you up."

Now, as I look back on all of these things that my mother would say to me, I understand the lessons that she was imparting to me.

So, I think it would be fair to say that, in many ways, I did complete her. But there was another person who'd once completed the picture. I did have a father, too.

My father, Bill McDonald, to whom she was married in 1960, was of Irish and German descent. In other words, as lily-white as anyone you could find.

My mother, meanwhile, was African-American and Cherokee—on her own mother's side, at least. As I have said, she never knew the identity of her father. Theories abound. Some people speculate that he was a son of the owner of the cotton plantation in South Carolina on which she was born. But it was assumed by almost everyone that her father had been white.

As a mixed-race child born out of wedlock, my mother was often made to feel ashamed of herself when she was growing up in the South. Her own mother soon abandoned her because the man she was going to marry didn't want "that yella gal," as mixed-race children were known there at the time. This was a rejection that my mother carried with her all her life. But my mother loved the fact that I was someone you couldn't pinpoint or pigeonhole in almost any respect.

"You are a walking United Nations!" she would frequently tell me with delight. "You either fill every quota or you break every rule."

You couldn't put me into any category. You couldn't identify my background. You couldn't say, "She's a white girl," or "She's a Black girl. She's Asian . . . Native American."

My mother herself was similarly hard to categorize or assign to any one group. She may have been Black to some people, but to others she wasn't Black enough. Growing up relatively light-skinned in the South, she wasn't quite dark-skinned enough to be considered Black by many people who were Black. Then, when she went up North, she wasn't white enough to be considered white. No one ever knew what to make of her.

There are letters in my mother's archives from people—both Black and white—saying incredibly nasty, horrible things to her. My mother kept all of these letters because they reminded her of who she was. "You think you're white." Or, "You think you're better than everybody." Or, "Who do you think you are?"

That is one of the many reasons she loved that no one knew quite how to identify me. She loved that you couldn't look at me and make a decision based strictly on my looks. You just didn't know, you know? It was left up to your imagination to figure out what I was.

My mother enjoyed having things left up to her own imagination. In fact, that was something else she was fond of saying. "I like to use the freedom of my own imagination."

She also was known to say to me, and others as well on many an occasion, "God may not be there when you want Him, but He's always on time."

She coined phrases like this so often that we began to refer to them as "Kittisms." Whether or not she was actually the first one to utter any of these expressions herself, she adopted them as a sort of mantra to such an extent that I have chosen to use them as chapter subtitles for this book.

But of all her sayings, one stands out in my mind the most by far. And not just in my *mind*. I have taken it to heart to such an extent that I have it tattooed on my wrist.

"Don't Panic."

It was something she said to me whenever I would begin to get so anxious about unsettling situations that I would forget to breathe.

It's what my own children still say to me now whenever I forget my mother's words and begin to stress out. No, what they actually say is, "Look at your wrist, Mom. Look at your wrist!"

And it was one of the many lessons I learned from my mother over our many years together, most memorably when we traveled to South Africa in 1974.

CHAPTER 2

Not a Walk in the Park

Never miss an opportunity to stay quiet.

As an internationally known entertainer, my mother performed all over the world. But being always a mother first, she hesitated to leave me behind. She also felt that seeing the world was a much better education than you could get in a classroom or from reading any book. It was the best way to learn about other people, cultures, and beliefs. You just can't get all of that from a book. So, when she was on the road, she usually took me along for the ride. From the day that I was born until the day that she died, first as mother/daughter and later with the added roles of entertainer/manager, we were rarely apart for more than a few days as we traveled the world together.

Our travels took us to many distant locales. I went almost everywhere with her, from Thailand and Tokyo to Morocco, Manilla, and Melbourne, and almost every place in between. But no trip was ever quite as memorable as the one that we made to South Africa in 1974, when I was twelve, which was considered to be a very controversial thing for anyone in the entertainment business to do at that time.

Many artists boycotted South Africa during that era because they didn't believe in its racially segregated system of Apartheid. My mother didn't believe in Apartheid either. But that didn't dissuade her from going there. On the contrary, it encouraged her to go. She felt that artists were the true diplomats, since they didn't need to abide by things like political correctness. That meant they had the ability to go places and effect change when politicians couldn't.

So my mother accepted an invitation to perform in South Africa, but on one condition. She stipulated that she would only perform for integrated audiences, something that was not done during that era.

She also had another agenda in making the trip. She hoped to use it to raise money to help build schools there for the African children. And by African children, I mean Black African children, not the white children who were referred to as "Afrikaans."

Now, being a celebrity, my mother was not only able to go to this racially segregated country, even though she was Black herself, but also to go with VIP status. That meant that she could travel anywhere in the country that she wanted to go while she was there. She essentially had free rein and wasn't going to be held to their laws of segregation.

So off we went to South Africa. And not just for a week or two. We stayed, as I recall, for what may have been as much as three months. We spent most of our time in Cape Town, because my mother had friends there.

While we were in Cape Town, the Royal Ballet happened to be performing there, too. And not just the Royal Ballet, but Margot Fonteyn. THE PRIMA BALLERINA OF THE ROYAL BALLET! She was my idol at the time because I dreamed of becoming a professional ballerina. Ah, to dream! I also dreamt of being a professional ice skater, a policewoman (on horseback), an FBI agent, and the CEO of a Fortune 500 company. I was going to lead a very busy life. But at that time, my No. 1 goal was to become a ballerina. So, of course, while I was there, I wanted to go see the one and only Margot Fonteyn dance.

My mother wasn't free to take me, though, because she was performing almost every night. So instead, my mother's friends took me to the Cape Town Opera House to see the ballet. We went in together and were walking around, then we went to find our seats. As we took our seats, many of the people around us began whispering, "Look! That's Eartha Kitt's daughter. That's Eartha Kitt's daughter!"

I was thinking, "Look at me! I'm this hot-shot little kid. Everyone knows who I am! How cool is that?" I mean, c'mon, you saw my list of dreams. I thought I was the bomb.

Then, the next day, someone showed my mother a local newspaper. One of the headlines read, "Eartha Kitt's Daughter Goes to Opera House." This was considered big news because the Opera House was for whites only. If I had been South African, I would have been considered "colored" because my mother was "colored." I wouldn't have been allowed inside. So, technically, I had broken the law. But because of my light skin coloring and blonde hair, and because I had walked in with a white family, nobody had questioned me.

Well, my mother thought this was the greatest thing ever. "My daughter broke the law!" she said proudly. Never mind that I hadn't known I was doing it. She proceeded to make a statement to the press about it, pointing out the ridiculousness of their rules and their Apartheid policies. But the story doesn't end there.

At the time, being of school age, I often traveled with a tutor—a British instructor, whom I really didn't like. Who wants to do schoolwork when you're traveling the world? But my life on the road wasn't all work and no play, even with a British tutor in tow. There was this really cool amusement park in Durban, South Africa, across the street from our hotel. And I was dying to go to it, so my tutor took me one day.

After that, I kept saying to my mother, "You have to come to the amusement park with us. It's so much fun!" This was something that I didn't ever get to do with her back in the U.S., because with her level of fame, it would have caused a major scene.

By the time I'd been born, my mother had already been famous for many years. As much as that may have brought certain privileges—such as getting to travel the world with her—there was also a downside to that. Having a famous mother meant that I couldn't do certain things. Or at least there were certain things that I couldn't do with *her*. Normal things, and also special things. Things that other kids I knew often got to do. Like go to the supermarket together. Or the circus. Or, above all else, Disneyland.

Growing up in California, I would have loved to go to Disneyland. But my mother couldn't have taken me. It would have been The Eartha Kitt Show, instead of a normal, "Take your daughter to Disneyland" trip. Back then, things weren't the way that they are today, where they have ways of making it easier for celebrities to go to popular places. Today, they'll offer public figures a VIP tour, for example. That wasn't the case back in the '60s. If you went somewhere like Disneyland, you went just like everybody else.

So I was dying to go to this amusement park in South Africa with my mother, where fewer people might recognize her. But her schedule was filled with interviews and rehearsals. She kept telling me, "I've got to work." But then one day she was finally free to take me to the amusement park.

By now, I had already been there a couple of times with my tutor. So as soon as we arrived, I led her straight to my favorite activity of all there, the bumper cars. The ride was about to start when all of a sudden, an Indian man who worked there came over and said to my mother, "Excuse me, ma'am. Are you European?"

My mother, as I said, had a very distinctive way of speaking, a unique accent that was hard for almost anyone to ever quite identify. But she certainly wasn't European.

"No," she said, "I'm American."

"That's not what I meant," the man replied. "What I meant is, are you colored?"

She looked up at this fellow, who had roughly the same complexion as she did, then down at her hands and her own dark skin. "Well," she said, "if you consider this colored, then yes, I guess I am."

From the time I was born, I had never really paid any attention to the difference in our complexions. People sometimes seemed baffled when trying to figure out how we were related. But I had never given much, if any, thought to the darker tone of my mother's skin, and that had never been an issue before. Why would it be now?

"I'm afraid you're going to have to leave, then," the man told her authoritatively. "This is a whites-only park. You're not allowed to be here."

Hearing this, my mother got up. She didn't say a word. She just stood up and got her bag, took me by the hand, and started to lead me out of the amusement park.

I couldn't believe this was happening.

"Tell him who you are!" I stage-whispered in her ear, totally amazed. "He doesn't know that you're a famous person, and that you have VIP status. That you're allowed to be in the park. You don't have to abide by the rules of this country. You're an American, and you're Eartha Kitt! Just tell him who you are!"

But she just looked at me, her face so stiff that it was almost frozen, like a mask. Then she said that thing that she always said.

Two things, in fact.

"Don't panic. God may not be there when you want Him, but He's always on time."

I wasn't just panicking now. I was crying because this was a very big deal to me. I realized that I was never going to go back there with her. We had just arrived, and this was the only time that she had been free to take me. I wanted to be in the park with my mother, and she was allowed to be there. Why didn't she just tell them who she was?

This was the budding teenager coming out in me. There were tears streaming down my face. Tears of outrage. Disbelief. Shame. But she was gripping my hand tightly as she remained absolutely calm. Almost eerily calm. Then she quietly led me out of the park without making any fuss.

But that's not how the story ends, either.

A day or two later, my mother was holding a press conference in our hotel when a photographer happened to say to her, "Miss Kitt, can we please get a picture of you standing out there on the balcony, with the amusement park in the background?"

As she happily obliged by stepping out onto the balcony, she replied, "You know, it's funny. I was thrown out of that amusement park just the other day."

"What!?!" almost everyone asked at once, as the room instantly erupted.

"Yes," she said, and she told the reporters the entire story.

It immediately made headlines that my mother had been kicked out of the amusement park. Now the owner of the park was being quoted in the newspapers, completely embarrassed that Eartha Kitt had been thrown off his property.

He soon came to her show with his wife and brought flowers and champagne to her dressing room. "How can I make it up to you?" he asked her. "My employee didn't know who you were. He didn't understand. Please accept my deepest apologies."

My mother didn't hesitate for one second. She was ready with an answer. "Well, we're building schools for African children, and if you could make a donation, that would be much appreciated."

She also dared to make an additional request. This one was on my behalf.

"Also, my daughter would really like me to be able to come back to the amusement park with her, and she would like to bring some of her friends."

"Anything you want!" the owner replied. "I'm sending you a check right now, and sending tickets, too. Six tickets? Eight? How many do you need? Bring as many people as you want. And please tell your daughter she can come as many times as she likes!"

The check arrived. The tickets, too. And what does my mother do? She gets two Black children, two white children, and two light-skinned "colored" children, and we walk into the park together. Now we've got an entourage of reporters and photographers following us, documenting the whole thing. We sit down on the bumper cars together, with all of these different-colored faces. And that's how my mother, in her own way, managed to help bring about change.

Whereas I would have been the hothead who would have stood up and made a big scene—saying, "Go get your boss! Don't you know who I am?"—my mother functioned on a different level. It wasn't that having this public embarrassment didn't cause her pain. I can only imagine how that humiliation must have made her feel. But she understood, deep inside her psyche, that she was going to have a much greater impact by holding her tongue and waiting than by standing on a soapbox and making a scene.

I think about these things often as I get older, and I think about the amount of strength that it must have taken to hold her emotions in check. I think about that type of rejection—about being told, "You can't do this," because of how you look. It was the kind of rejection that she had faced early in life and that she never quite recovered from, no matter what she did, how many shows she performed, or how famous she became.

My mother was really a part of history—American history, entertainment history, world history, and certainly Black history. She happened to be a famous person. There are lots of people whose names you may never have heard who also effected change.

I'm just saying that my mother, and so many others—all the Rosa Parkses of the world, and many anonymous people, too—were able to keep their heads up high and to stay strong. My mother did that. I saw her do it with my own eyes.

She was this fascinating person. And I find myself becoming more and more fascinated by her and by her ability and inner strength—her strength to speak up, and also her strength to keep quiet, because doing that may take the most strength of all. She would often say to me, "Never miss an opportunity to stay quiet."

I was recounting this story to someone recently, and I remembered a pond at my mother's house in Connecticut, and how she taught me to skip stones there. The big stones don't skip very far, she showed me. They have a ripple effect, but they just go plop.

My mother then explained to me, "See, when a big stone drops into the water, it creates big ripples on the shoreline. But if you take a little rock, a very thin one, and you skim it across the water, see how it makes a tiny little ripple? Well, those ripples have an effect on the shoreline as well. Maybe not as big an effect, or as quick an effect. But over time, all of those little ripples start to build up. And you will see change happen."

My mother had the pleasure of being recognized during her lifetime for her many talents. But after her passing, it has become apparent not only how much of her work has passed the test of time, but also how much of a trailblazer she was and how many generations of people she touched and impacted and continues to inspire today.

She genuinely came from nothing and raised herself up by sheer will and relentless effort. She unabashedly spoke her mind and unequivocally supported the underdog. And although she had little in the way of formal education, she had so much wisdom—kernels of truth that would benefit so many people that I cannot keep them to myself.

She had no idea how that incident in Durban, South Africa, was going to pan out in the end. Having experienced extreme deprivation herself, she was always prepared to defend those who suffered from poverty, discrimination, or rejection, whoever they might be. But my mother understood instinctively, on a very deep level, that even when your voice is known and loved throughout the world, sometimes it's better to simply hold your tongue.

She also understood that when an opportunity arises to help others, or to create change, no matter how small it may be, it only takes one person to make a difference. One person who doesn't panic, even if she *is* just a poor cotton picker from the South.

One person, with possibly a little help from God, who may not be there when you want Him, but who is always on time.

CHAPTER 3

No Ordinary Life

I like to use the freedom of my own imagination.

Life with Eartha was never dull. Far from it! From the moment I was born, I was always by my mother's side (or, more accurately, as an infant, in her arms). Always a hands-on parent, she was reluctant to ever leave me in the care of others while she performed throughout the world. That meant that even as a young child, I was exposed to glamorous nightclubs and the theater. I was repeatedly whisked away to live in London, Las Vegas, or other distant locales, reluctantly at times as I got older.

So instead of singing "I'm Still Here," as my mother so often did, my signature tune could have been called, "I'll *Stay* Here." And by "here," I would have meant home. Not that my home life was all that ordinary, either. My mother, you see, was not only famous. She was also famously unconventional. Even by Hollywood standards. And so, what I often craved was the typical stuff that other kids had. Attending public school. Riding my bike around the neighborhood. Junk food. (Ah, junk food! That's for another chapter . . .)

I was born in Los Angeles, in what was then called Cedars of Lebanon Hospital, on November 26, 1961. The house that I grew up in was a sprawling, Mediterranean-style structure in Beverly Hills, set on 2½ acres of land. My mother bought that house in 1957 for $90,000. It was a lot of money for a house at that time. Her accountants and business advisors thought she was crazy to pay so much for a piece of property located up in "the Hills." But she followed her instincts, as was always her way, and bought it anyway.

Truth be known, she was happy to have found it at all. She had repeatedly struck out in the sections of Bel Air and Beverly Hills in which she had originally been looking. Residents there were not quite ready to put out the welcome mat for an African American neighbor. Even a world-famous one.

The house was situated on a cul-de-sac, nestled right in the hills themselves. It had citrus trees, a huge garden, and an aviary. For a cotton picker from South Carolina, it was a little slice of secluded heaven. The swimming pool, pool house, and separate guest house it also included may make it sound more lavish than it was, because my mother wasn't someone who went in for "show-offy" things. She was surprisingly very simple in her tastes. With the given name Eartha, land was important to my mother. She felt that owning real estate was far more important than having diamonds or furs because, as she would say, "They aren't making any more of it." She also felt that "land gives you stability," and a means of survival, if needed.

The house stood at the end of a winding private road. The entire street had once been an old estate, but it had since been divided up. My mother bought the parcel that had been the stables. (How appropriately down-to-earth is that?) Although she had the place totally redesigned, she maintained the original structure, keeping its rustic roots on display, almost to make a statement as to the importance of farm life. It was shaped like a giant rectangle, with an open interior courtyard. One side of the house, which served as our dining room, had three stalls with the names of the horses that had once occupied them— Lefty, Tyro, and Priscilla—still carved into the double-hung doors. The house itself was red brick with a terracotta tile roof. Very California style.

And very *down-to-Eartha.*

The only problem for me, as a child, was that it was a little remote. Since I went to private school, and Los Angeles is so spread out, I didn't have any friends who were close by. And living behind iron gates on a cul-de-sac, there were never any neighborhood children knocking on our door asking, "Can Kitt come out and play?" Sometimes I would ride my bike around in circles on the driveway, or play hopscotch and tetherball in the yard all alone. But that was OK. As an only child, I liked being alone.

I knew my mother's stories of her early life in South Carolina, where she had spent much of her time in the woods with the animals, watching and learning from them as they foraged for food and went about their days. She would often say how she liked being by herself; how being alone gave her a sense of freedom. So, for me, it felt acceptable to be on my own. It seemed perfectly normal. My mother never said to me, "Why don't you go ask so-and-so if she can play?" She never said that, in part, because I never said I was bored. My mother never heard those two words from me: "I'm bored!" For I never *was* bored. As an only child, you learn to entertain yourself.

And my mother encouraged me to be creative and nurtured my vivid imagination. When she played Caesars Palace in Las Vegas, I would run around with my little dog, exploring the nooks and crannies of the hotel. I was like a kid in a candy store, running around—or, more often, dancing with abandon—through its halls and open spaces. (Yes, times were different then. I was known to many of the employees, and my mother made sure they were watching out for me at all times.)

Similarly, when I was home, I would venture into the woods and hills of my backyard, inventing wild scenarios and stories in my head. Our property was lush with California foliage, and my mother had created these paths that zigzagged up and down, connecting the different levels of the property like a well-mapped maze. She'd had a glassed-in writing studio built at the top, and you could see a lot of Los Angeles from there. If you stood on the very tips of your toes, you could also see the ocean, she said, although my toes never seemed quite long enough for that.

I could often be found up there undertaking all sorts of adventures with our two dogs—a big white standard poodle named Snowball, and Baba, our little apricot-colored miniature poodle, whom I had named myself when I was two. They were my trusty sidekicks and forever playmates. Together we might be pirates, or go off on an adventure in the Amazon jungle.

As an avid reader, I would create my own live-action versions of Nancy Drew and The Hardy Boys mysteries. Or short dramatic reenactments of other favorite books like *Wuthering Heights* and *Jane Eyre*. I loved playing by myself because I could make up all the rules. I could also play all of the parts. And the part that I always chose to play was that of The Hero of my story.

I was never a princess. Never a damsel in distress. I was the one conquering lands or slaying dragons. I was always a strong, Joan of Arc-type leader, out blazing a trail, because that was the female role model I saw every day—the woman who taught me to rely on my instincts and always follow my heart. My mother! That was who she was, and that was my life, too. She had given me the freedom and the confidence to invent and explore. I never felt that I needed someone to come rescue me. I was perfectly capable of being the rescuer myself.

I rarely watched television. I really didn't need to. From the time that I was old enough to walk, I had my own imagination to entertain myself and keep me busy. I would spend hours and hours out with the dogs, exploring the landscape and the foliage. I was content just to be, enjoying my own company.

I'm still perfectly content with my own company to this day. My husband often comes home from playing golf, and I'll be sitting outside all by myself. No book, no music, no television, no noise whatsoever. "What are you doing?" he'll ask.

"Oh, nothing," I'll say.

"What do you mean, 'nothing?'" he'll ask. "What are you looking at?"

"Nothing. Just the trees." I attribute that mostly to my having had a mother who encouraged me to embrace who I was, and to think for myself. She bred story-telling. Thanks to her, I too like to use the freedom of my own imagination.

My mother felt that nobody could constrain your dreams. Nobody could tell you not to imagine something. They might tell you, "You cannot become that. You can't do that. It's not appropriate. It's not possible," or whatever else the reasoning behind your not doing something might be. But, she would emphasize, no one can stop you from imagining yourself doing whatever YOU wish.

You can get lost in your own imagination. You can be anything you want to be. You can go anywhere you want to go. You can accomplish anything you want to do.

My mother didn't merely say these things. She never once stopped me from doing anything. Rather, she conveyed quite the opposite. So when I went up into the hills, whether I was pretending to be the Queen of Sheba or an astronaut rocketing to Mars, or maybe a gun-slinging cowboy riding the open range,

ANYTHING was possible in my mind. And, subsequently, possible in life!

I was very independent from an early age. My mother had been, too, but not for the same reasons. She wasn't given confidence as a child. She wasn't given freedom. She had learned to be independent because she couldn't rely on anyone else. When she had gone into the woods, it wasn't to play. It was because she needed to hide. She needed to find a place where it was safe.

CHAPTER 4

Southern Hell

The present without the past has nothing to say for itself.

My mother didn't have the luxury of feeling safe or secure as a child. Her early years were anything but that. I learned about the mistreatment she experienced starting from when I was very young. She wouldn't necessarily tell all of these stories to me directly. But she would recount them in interviews, and I was never far from her side. Sitting on the floor playing with my toys, whether in a hotel suite or at home, I was always listening to her share what her life was like growing up. When you hear all these tales, even as a small child, you begin to understand early on who your mother is.

And in *my* mother's case, the stories were very intense.

You know that old book, *All I Really Need to Know I Learned in Kindergarten?* Well, everything that my mother really needed to know, she learned in the South.

My mother was born Eartha Mae Keith (pronounced "keet") on a cotton plantation, in a little town called North, South Carolina. Her mother's family were poor sharecroppers—tenant farmers who forfeited a portion of their crops to the plantation owners as rent. Her mother was named Anna Mae Keith, the family having adopted the last name of the Swiss-German people who owned the plantation. When my mother later saw the name written, though, it was spelled "Kitt." A mixture of Native American and African American, Anna Mae was only about sixteen, and unmarried, when my mother was born. My mother always assumed that she herself had probably been conceived by rape. It wasn't common knowledge who her father was. She would never learn his name. Several possibilities have been bandied about over the years. Some people say he was a son of the owner of the plantation on which she was born. Others believe he may have been a local doctor, an older man for whom her mother was sent to work after his wife had died. Yet one thing that was always assumed was that he had been white.

Being both illegitimate and of mixed race, my mother was treated as an outcast by almost everyone around. The lighter complexion of her skin soon led to her being abandoned as well. A few years after she was born, Anna Mae met an older man who wanted to marry her. But he already had children of his own and said that he would wed her on one condition—that she leave little Eartha

Mae behind. One of my mother's earliest memories was of seeing her mother kneeling before him, tearfully begging him to reconsider, only to be told, "I don't want 'that yella gal' in my house."

So, at the tender age of only perhaps five or six, she was left with a family she did not know. She referred to the woman who took her in as "Aunt Rosa." But it was clear that Aunt Rosa was not an actual aunt. She was also no kind of mother. She proceeded to treat my mother like a Southern version of Cinderella. She forced her to wash the dishes, slop the pigs, feed the chickens, clean the house, and build a fire in the fireplace every day after sweeping the old ashes out—never mind that my mother was barely more than a toddler at the time. Meanwhile, this woman dressed her in rags and nearly starved her, feeding her only leftover scraps that she was expected to share with the family's pets and animals.

"I wished I'd had it as good as Cinderella," my mother would say to me. "That family treated their animals better than they treated me."

The woman's teenage grandchildren, who lived with her as well, did even worse. On many occasions, my mother recounted, they tied her to a tree, pulled down her pants, and beat her with a switch until her bare bottom was covered with welts and blood ran down her legs. But my mother never uttered a word about it to anyone. That would have been the quickest way to who knows where? And who was going to believe a "yella gal," anyway?

Most heartbreaking of all for her was that her mother never came back for her. Rather, Anna Mae died within a year or two, when she was only in her early twenties, under suspicious circumstances.

My mother believed that she had been poisoned, although that was pure speculation on her part. Anna Mae had apparently been served a meal topped with a mysterious red powder and abruptly fallen ill, never to recover. My mother told me that when her mother was on her deathbed, someone took my mother to see Anna Mae for the very last time. I guess they knew that she didn't have long to live, and somebody said, "That girl should be allowed to say goodbye."

There was also a baby who had been born to her mother and was probably still under a year old at the time. My mother witnessed a type of ritual in which the other women there passed this baby back and forth over her mother's body several times. This was presumably a custom popular in the South known as "shaking off the spirit," meant to prevent the dead person's spirit from inhabiting the body of the baby. I don't know if that scene truly happened or not. I don't know if *any* of it is true. But my mother certainly believed it, and carried that memory throughout her life.

Now genuinely motherless, my mother began laboring out in the cotton fields, despite being just a child. It was backbreaking work, she told me, but little children were relatively good at it because they were closer to the ground than adults. By 1930, cotton prices had plummeted to below 10 cents a pound, but she spoke with pride of having been able to pick enough to earn a whole dollar in a single day. The stems of a cotton branch are pointed, she said, and it was easy to prick your fingers on them. That made the work even more difficult because you certainly couldn't hand in bushels stained with blood.

Missing school was not an issue for her. School for Black children in her town, held in a one-room shack on the grounds of a local church, was in session only when there was no farm work to be done, meaning only a few months of the year. And my mother was rarely able to attend even then. She didn't have enough clothes to wear, and those that she did have were so ragged that, even in this dirt-poor area, the other children would ridicule her about them.

But then, one day, salvation seemingly arrived. It appeared in the form of a box full of clothing, along with a train ticket to travel north. Someone from the South had apparently alerted an aunt who lived in New York City about how badly my mother was being treated. "If you don't get this child out of here, they're going to kill her," she had been told. "Or she's just going to die from abuse." So the aunt sent for her.

Having no suitcase, my mother was put onto the train dressed in every piece of clothing that had been mailed to her, layered one over the other. From the way that she would describe the scene, I could picture this little urchin barely able to walk because she was wearing so many clothes. She was sitting on a big train, terrified about where she might be headed, clinging to the first real treat that she had ever received, a paper bag containing a catfish sandwich on white bread, an apple, and a slice of sweet potato pie. Whatever time of year it was, I can only imagine that she must have been incredibly hot!

This aunt who had come to her rescue *was* an actual relative. She may have saved my mother from a life of pain and suffering, but motherly skills she did not possess either.

Aunt Mamie was a "spinster"—that was the word my mother used when referring to her—and never having had any children of her own, she didn't know what to do with a small child. She appeared to have taken my mother in out of a sense of family obligation, or "Christian duty," rather than genuine good will or affection. And even though the aunt had a job, she, too, barely gave my mother enough to eat. She was also so severely strict, to the point of being abusive, that there were many times my mother ran away.

Whenever my mother would recount these memories from her childhood, which she continued to do throughout her life, it was always as if she were reliving every painful incident. Painful for her. And painful for me. When I would hear her talk about being treated badly as a child, it was almost as if I were experiencing it myself as well, because I could feel her pain.

As a little girl, all I really wanted was to make my mother feel better. But as time went on, I began to wonder why she was holding onto those memories and couldn't just move on.

"Let go of it already!" I would say to her, especially as I got older. "That's enough! How long are you going to hang on to this anger and pain—the mistreatment that you suffered from this person or that person in the South?"

I think the honest answer was that she couldn't let go of the past. I think she was afraid to. Letting go would have meant that she wouldn't be who she was anymore.

"Why would I want to forget?" she would ask. "Why would I want to let go of something that was such an integral part of the foundation that made me who I am?"

Yet she was not someone who had been defeated by the adversity that she had faced. Not in the least. On the contrary, if anything, it actually gave her a sense of pride. It served as incontrovertible proof of how incredibly strong she was inside. She wasn't going to let them defeat her. She wasn't ever going to let anyone do her in.

Besides, even though she held onto the pain, and it was easy for her to recall what it had been like back then—as clearly as if it were yesterday—she wasn't bitter. She was never a bitter person.

"I have taken all the manure that has been thrown on me and used it as fertilizer," she would say. A true "Kittism" if there ever was one.

My mother loved life! She would wake up every single morning and say, "Thank you, God, for allowing me to open my eyes and see the beauty that surrounds me."

She had grown up being exploited and mistreated, and yet she had always been able to appreciate every leaf, flower, and cloud in the sky. That was where she found peace. In the woods. Alone with Nature. The animals didn't judge her for being different. They didn't mistreat her because she was illegitimate. They didn't hold her being an orphan against her. My mother, Eartha, was truly "of the Earth." Nature was where she felt connected. Throughout her life, being in the outdoors was always a priority for her. Being close to the dirt, she would say, was where she felt the most "at home." The irony of that statement should not be lost on any of us.

I learned from her the importance of being grateful for every day. *Be grateful.* Smile and laugh! For every day is a gift. Every day is a blessing.

CHAPTER 5

Life Up North

The only thing I can sell and still own is my talent.

The train ride north that she took at age eight turned out to literally be her ticket up. After the rural South, New York City, with its skyscrapers and traffic—not to mention electric lights and indoor plumbing—was a jaw-dropping revelation for my mother. The first time she needed to use the bathroom in her aunt's apartment, she was directed to go inside this little room, but had no idea what to do once inside. She sat on the edge of the bathtub afraid to ask an adult for help because asking for anything was something that she had learned not to do back in the South. She thought she was being punished until, finally, when she had been gone for way too long, her aunt came in, saw her distress, and explained that "outhouses" were no longer where she would go to "take care of her business."

But life "up North," as my mother called it, did not prove to be heaven on earth. Far from it. Her aunt, who lived in Harlem, provided her with shelter, clothing, and food, but didn't exactly lavish her with affection or attention. Rather, she all but ignored her, but also could be harsh to the point of getting violent. She yelled at her, slapped her, and sometimes even beat her. Once, convinced that my mother had taken a box of chocolates—a gift from her aunt's boyfriend that the aunt had simply misplaced—she beat her savagely with the cord of an electric iron, giving her a black eye.

Things only got worse as my mother became a teenager. Aunt Mamie, being deeply religious, ordered her repeatedly to stay away from boys. Never mind that my mother was "a good girl," and had never even been kissed. "You'll have a baby and bring shame on me," her aunt kept warning her. "I'd have to take care of both of you! Then what would I do?"

To make matters worse, my mother was also bullied at school. But she found that she loved school and learning. She not only excelled in her studies, but gradually began to attract attention for her singing, acting, and public speaking abilities. The child who had learned that it was safer to stay silent in North, South Carolina, slowly began to find her voice in Harlem, New York. One of her junior high school teachers, sensing her potential, arranged for her to audition at what is now the Fiorello H. LaGuardia High

School of Music & Art and Performing Arts, and she quickly was accepted.

"I starred in many plays both in church and in school," she recalled in her 1976 autobiography *Alone with Me*. "And the more I acted, the more word got to my aunt that I was 'a great little actress.' 'You must encourage her,' people kept telling my aunt. And the more I overheard these remarks, the more I expected my aunt to praise me and encourage me. But I got no encouragement from her. Absolutely none. When she came to see me in a church play. . . . We'd walk home in silence. I'd wait for her to make some comment about the play, perhaps tell me whether she thought me good or not. Nothing."

One teacher, though, a woman named Mrs. Banks, noticed both her talent and the unmistakable signs of trouble in her life. She not only reassured her, but also gave her a matinee ticket to see José Ferrer perform in the play *Cyrano de Bergerac*. It was a life-changing experience. During a 2005 interview with Charles Osgood on *CBS Sunday Morning*, my mother recalled seeing the adulation that the audience had given the actor.

"I thought, 'I want to get that kind of love and affection,'" she said. "And when I left the theater, I walked through Central Park, back to 115th Street, longing for somebody to care about me like that."

The true turning point for her, though, came when, on a dare from a friend, my mother auditioned for famed choreographer and modern dancer Katherine Dunham, the director of a prestigious all-Black dance company (comparable to the popular Alvin

Ailey American Dance Theater of today). She was soon granted a full scholarship to study at Dunham's prestigious dance school. As a member of the Dunham Dancers, my mother would tour throughout the U.S., Mexico, and Europe. It may have seemed like fate was suddenly in her favor, but success for my mother was never just a matter of luck. She put in the time. She put in the effort. She followed her instincts.

And she had a plan.

"It's important to learn everybody's part," my mother would always say to me. "You learn how to make the costumes, how to play the instruments, and what everyone else's dance is, because you never know when you may have to step into that role." Some people may say that sounds very opportunistic. But I think she was just being realistic. She came from nothing, and she had been living at the lowest level possible when, for the first time, she had been presented with an opportunity to rise. For her, this wasn't about financial success. It was about being successful on so many levels. But, mostly, it was about being prepared.

She was always prepared to take on any role, or fill any gap that opened up. And that's exactly what she did after she got into an argument with Katherine Dunham one day.

They were in Paris, and my mother had been asked to perform on her own, at a nightclub, on her night off. Miss Dunham wouldn't allow her to do it, though. My mother couldn't understand that. She didn't see anything wrong with trying something new during her free time. But Miss Dunham remained adamantly against it. She dared her to leave the company if she wanted to pursue her own aspirations, and my mother took that dare. I don't think she took it thinking, "I'm going to show *you!*" No, a door had opened, and she felt, "I've got to go through it."

She didn't have an act, though. Didn't have a set of songs to perform. Didn't even have a costume. So she went out and bought a piece of fabric with the little bit of money that she had saved, and she sewed herself a dress. Then she went to the nightclub, the Café du Paris.

"What's your act?" the man in charge asked her.

"I don't know," my mother said. "I'll figure it out."

"What do you sing?" he asked. Again, she didn't know.

All she knew was that this was the door that was open in front of her. And that when a door opens up for you, you go through it, one foot in front of the other.

That was when she began developing this persona that evolved over time. She told me that it happened out of fear, beginning that very first night in that Paris nightclub. Never having sung solo in public before, she just stood there as the band began playing, not sure what to do. But she knew French, so she started speaking it, apprehensively and quietly at first, and that, slowly, became her act—a sort of sex kitten attitude, this "look but don't touch" image.

What began from fear gradually evolved over time. My mother had a natural ability to hold somebody's attention strictly with her eyes. That, along with the unique quality of her voice, captivated people. They didn't understand it, but they were mesmerized by it, and they wanted more.

After her debut at the Café du Paris, she was booked to do singing engagements in London and Istanbul. Not long after that, back in New York, she appeared at The Village Vanguard, followed by another club called The Blue Angel, where Broadway producer Leonard Sillman discovered her and put her in his latest musical production *New Faces of 1952*. In this, she drew raves as she began to hone and perfect her blatantly seductive, provocative, yet blasé stage image, with a sultry, show-stopping rendition of a song that had been written just for her called "Monotonous," written by Arthur Siegel.

She performed this world-weary number, describing an array of extravagant things that completely bored her, using her own inspiration for choreography, posing sensuously on a series of chaise lounges arranged strategically across the stage.

That show was a huge hit and was followed by a national tour, and then a film version from Twentieth Century Fox. Broadway stardom led to an RCA recording contract and a succession of best-selling records, including "Love for Sale," "I Want to Be Evil," "Santa Baby" (the best-selling Christmas song of 1953), and "Folk Tales of the Tribes of Africa," which earned her a Grammy nomination.

By the time I was born, my mother had also earned her first Tony nomination, starred in *The Mark of the Hawk* with Sidney Poitier, *Anna Lucasta* with Sammy Davis Jr., and *St. Louis Blues* with Nat King Cole and Cab Calloway, and had been honored with her own star on the Hollywood Walk of Fame.

CHAPTER 6

Love Not for Sale

Don't do me any favors. The price is too costly.

I s your name Kitt Kitt?"

I'm often asked that question—if that was the name I was born with. Of course not! My given name is Kitt McDonald. My father's name was William McDonald. He was not some wealthy industrialist or famous figure from the world of entertainment.

Nope. My dad was more or less just a regular Joe.

How did some regular guy from Evanston, Illinois, meet and marry an international sex symbol? The answer is a complicated story.

Soon after my mother left the Dunham Dancers for the Café du Paris, she was discovered by Orson Welles. Rumors were that she was romantically involved with him. But my mother always claimed that their relationship was strictly platonic. Yes, there was that one night in Paris when he bit her lip in the course of a passionate kiss; bit it so hard that it bled. But that happened on stage, during a performance, when she was playing Helen of Troy opposite Welles in *Time Runs*, his own adaptation of the Faust story. She always insisted that he was just her director and co-star, as well as her mentor and not-so-secret admirer. Nothing more than that.

I don't know. I wasn't there.

The first real relationship that my mother had was with a man named Charlie, a young stagehand who was on tour in Mexico with the Dunham Dancers. But he already had a fiancé back home, and they chose to keep their romance totally under wraps. He also knew that his white family would never have accepted her. After it was over, she carried a torch for him for years.

"I have since learned that I don't fall in love easily, but when I do it takes the kick of a mule to set me straight again," she later wrote.

The next man of note in her life was John Barry Ryan III, a young banking heir. She met him while performing at the Blue Angel in New York. He came to her show nightly for weeks before summoning the nerve to speak to her. And then what he had to say was much more than merely "hello."

"I know all about you," he told her. "You never have to worry about anything again as long as you live. I will take care of you." Before long, they became inseparable.

He showered her with lavish gifts, including an emerald ring surrounded by diamonds and her first mink stole. "It's the only way I know to say I love you," he said.

But this was in the early 1950s, and Ryan was white. Not only did they receive disapproving stares from strangers on the street, but they also began to be criticized by both the Black and white press, not just for their difference in race but also in social class.

"I was reprimanded by the black press for my relationship with the 'downtown' world," she wrote, referring to the primarily white social circles south of Harlem. "And we were both scorned by the downtown press for not conforming to society's game."

Far more significant was that his family did not approve of the interracial match. His well-connected mother arranged to have him leave the country to serve as assistant director on a John Huston film shooting in Egypt. When he returned, Ryan told my mother that it was over between them, and then he soon married someone else.

A similar scenario ensued when, a few years later, she was introduced to MGM Studios heir Arthur Loew Jr. after her show at the Mocombo, a Los Angeles hotspot. Once again, it was love at first sight.

"Loew was my kind of man; a man with a wonderful sense of humour, a traveled man, a man who was aware; a curious man, intelligent and fun," she would write. He returned to see her perform nightly, and also returned her affection.

"At last I had found someone who would be with me forever," she thought.

Or had she?

They became known as an item in the press. His overbearing mother, though, was not impressed.

I have no doubt that Arthur Loew was truly the love of my mother's life. But his socialite mother wouldn't allow them to marry because my mother was a "Negro," as African Americans were referred to then. That, I think, really broke my mother's heart; that he either couldn't or wouldn't stand up to his parents. It seemed that it was more important for him to stay a Loew than it was to have my mother as his wife.

After he broke it off, their mutual friend James Dean—yes, *the* James Dean, star of such iconic films as *Rebel Without a Cause* and *East of Eden,* whom my mother was very close with and always referred to as "Jamie"—filled in the demoralizing details. He told her that Loew's mother had apparently put her foot down firmly, stating, "'He will marry that girl over my dead body.'"

At least there was no disapproving mother to contend with when she met cosmetics mogul Charles Revson, the founder of Revlon. But there was a wife, albeit a soon-to-be-ex one.

My mother was invited to a party he threw while she was performing in Puerto Rico. Revson, who was twenty years older than my mother, handed her his card. She would later summon the nerve to call him.

"I still did not know at the time that Mr. Revson *was* Revlon," she would say. He told her that he was separated from his wife, but was locked in a heated divorce and custody battle. The next day he sent her a gold bracelet, followed by other posh gifts.

Receiving presents was nice. But what she really craved was love and a stable relationship.

Eventually, with pressure from Revson's estranged wife, who was threatening to expose "his black mistress," their romance began to crumble. My mother didn't want to be anyone's mistress. She wanted to be important enough to be someone's wife.

By now, she had realized that what she really desired most was a family of her own. ". . . to be fulfilled as a woman, to feel and know what that fulfillment really meant . . ."

And that's when my father, Bill McDonald, came into the picture.

CHAPTER 7

Father *Doesn't* Know Best

I know myself. I don't know you.
Therefore, I trust myself more than I trust you.

One night in 1958, on a plane from Las Vegas to LA, my mother had met an actor named Bob Dix. He later introduced her to his friend Bill McDonald. "Bob was an extremely handsome guy, who attracted girls like flies to honey," she would later recall, "and Bill caught the overflow." Bill, who was studying accounting at the University of Southern California, later became a CPA and associate at an LA real-estate investment firm. He began to visit my mother at the new home she had just bought in Beverly Hills.

"Bill was all right to have around for a few laughs, but he was nothing to fall in love with," she felt. He was physically strong, though, intelligent, and not bad to look at. And although he, too, was white, and from a well-to-do family, he had something else compelling to offer: a mother who not only accepted my mother, but also was prepared to embrace her as part of the family. Having suffered abandonment at an early age, then been rejected by the mother of nearly every man that she had ever loved, she yearned for this kind of validation even more than she had once hungered for enough food to eat.

It may sound surprising that after all of the illustrious and well-known men my mother had dated, she ended up with someone who was an accountant. A regular guy. But there was a sense of stability in that. And, at the age of thirty-three, she was more than ready to settle down. And so, when Bill proposed to her, she eagerly accepted. They were married on June 9, 1960.

It was a small wedding held at my mother's house, performed by a Superior Court judge. She wore a tasteful and rather modest-looking, pale mint-colored, tea-length chiffon dress trimmed in satin by costume designer Don Loper, with a matching pillbox hat, short veil, silk shoes, and bag. I remember her outfit so clearly because it hung in her closet, immaculately preserved, for years. As a little girl, I would take it out and dance around the room holding it up to me, dreaming, as most little girls do, of my own wedding dress. As the years went by, I became more and more impressed at how my mother always remained capable of still fitting into it. Taller and bigger than she was, I never did get into it myself.

By the time I was born, though, in November of 1961, there were already issues in their marriage. I'm not sure what first made the relationship between them start to unravel. But my mother soon began to harbor a fair amount of anger and resentment toward my father.

My father had served in Korea and come back from the war severely wounded. He had stepped on a landmine and lost two fingers, a portion of his stomach, and part of the back of his head. He underwent twenty-five different surgeries and remained in pain for the rest of his life. As a result, he gradually became addicted to opioids.

I often think now about what his military experience must have been like for him. My father went to war as an eighteen-year-old, having been drafted, and he came back at age twenty or twenty-one completely destroyed—emotionally, mentally, and physically. I'm sure he never received much, if any, psychological therapy afterwards, though, something that he clearly needed, and which presumably might have helped.

But who paid any attention to post traumatic stress disorder at that time? The term "PTSD" itself wasn't even coined or officially classified as a condition until 1980. Similarly, who connected prescription drugs with substance abuse back in those days? No one. After you had surgery, you were in pain, so you were given medication for it. In time, my father became a full-fledged addict. At some point later in his life, he even became a dealer, I believe. The reality is that I didn't get to know him all that well.

As a little girl, I wanted to have this fairytale family. Both a mother and a father. And the fantasy that my parents would be together. We would be walking down the street, and they'd be holding my hands, one on either side of me. But that certainly wasn't the reality. And as I got older, that wasn't even the reality I wanted with him.

My father, you see, could be incredibly blunt. Which can be a good trait, but oftentimes is not. For example, if you were to meet him for the first time, you would probably offer the usual niceties, asking, "How are you?" Well, he didn't understand why people would automatically ask how you were when they didn't really care to know, or at the very least weren't really interested in a truthful response.

Maybe he was right. But it can be very disconcerting and shocking when someone doesn't adhere to social norms, even if those norms are somewhat meaningless. Well, that someone was my father. He was one of those socially uncomfortable people, like Larry David on his TV show *Curb Your Enthusiasm*. If you asked, "How are you?" he would proceed to tell you in excruciating detail how he was. Or he might give you a hard time and reply, "Why are you asking? Is that something you really want to know?"

Because of his heavy involvement with drugs, I think my mother was probably wise to limit my exposure to him. My father was never a big part of my life. But that was not completely his choice. For as much as she would complain that it was he who didn't make much of an effort to participate in my life, the truth was that she felt compelled to protect me from him. There was no need for me to be exposed to his lifestyle and his vitriol, she believed. I mean, there was no upside. That, at least, is what she must have thought.

Now, though, seeing the important influence that fathers have on their little girls—because I look at my own daughter and how her father sets the tone for so much in her life—I look back and realize that I really missed out by not having that in my life. Even if I understand my mother's concerns and her desire to "keep me safe."

In any case, my father died over a decade ago, but by that point I hadn't seen him for many years.

ABOVE: A rare portrait of
my parents. RIGHT: My
mother performing in
London in 1962.

My father with his parents before he was deployed to Korea.

My mother with my paternal grandmother, Nora. Their bond was everlasting.

ABOVE: My mother at her baby shower, with Grandma Nora making sure all goes well.
BELOW: My parents soon after bringing me home from the hospital.

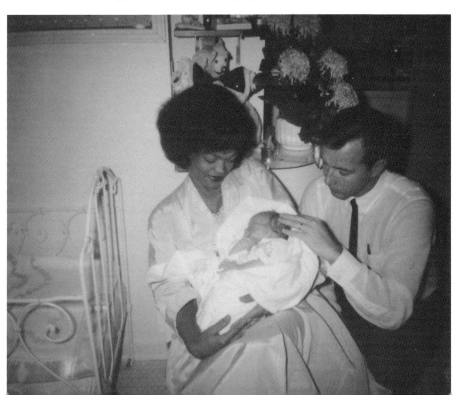

ABOVE: Christening time. BELOW: It may be just a photo shoot, but
my mother could always find a way to fit in a workout.

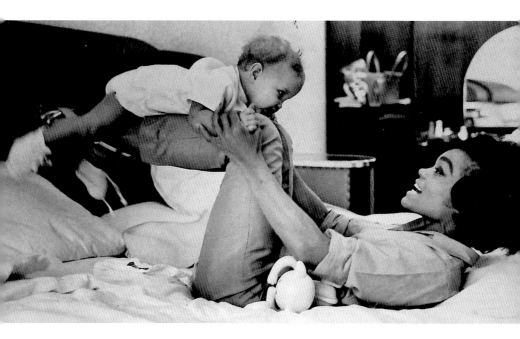

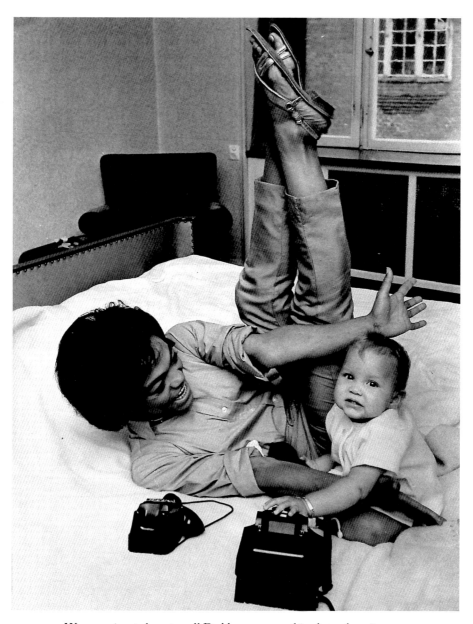

We are going to have to call Daddy as soon as this photo shoot is over.

My grandmother and aunts often accompanied us on tour.
(Left to right: Grandma Nora, Aunt Evelyn holding me,
my mother, and Jean Pomier, a family friend)

ABOVE: Me with my parents and our standard poodle Snowball at our house in Beverly Hills.

LEFT: My parents share a cerebral moment.

From the moment
the doctor said I could
get on a plane, my mother
and I took flight.

CHAPTER 8

Scenes from a Marriage

*The feelings I have for you are etched
upon my heart and soul.*

My parents' marriage started off well enough, as I said, but it was not built to last. It was so brief, in fact, and so profoundly disappointing to my mother, that in her entire 276-page book *Alone with Me*, my father only merited two short paragraphs, one of which focused more on me than on him.

"I can't speak for Bill, but I was immeasurably enriched by our union; I have my daughter, who's truly the sunshine of my life, and I found a close friend in my late mother-in-law, whom I adored."

My mother was deeply attached to my paternal grandmother, Nora. As for her feelings for my father, or lack thereof, she grew to resent him and his limited involvement in my life (even if she did play a role in that) so much that later in life, she often referred to him as "the sperm donor." (Not her finest moment.)

But I do think that my mother did love my father at one point. Truly loved him. Unfortunately, as she got further away from this point, her original feelings for him became less apparent to her.

I recently discovered a treasure trove of letters that they left behind—reams of mail that passed between them, almost daily, starting from when they first met. And these tattered old letters tell a very different story. There was a touching, unmistakable devotion between them (albeit strangely formally worded at times) that I never actually witnessed.

Take the four-page dispatch that my father sent to my mother dated December 15, 1960, six months after they were married. "Dear Wife," it begins (and yes, I find that a little funny, too). Then, about halfway through, it states, "Love you. In fact, love you madly, in fact more than madly, but I don't want you to get carried away with how much I love you so I won't say any more. Until later of course." It concludes, "Love you. Miss you. Love you. Miss you. Love you. Miss you. And everything else. Next year I promise we will spend the holidays together. Love you much, much, much, much, much."

Does that sound like a mere "sperm donor" to you?

Even more overwrought is a letter that he had sent to her earlier that year, on July 4, when she was performing in Scotland. It contained these impassioned words:

Most people aren't even remotely aware of the depth of my love for you. Many reasons have been brought forth as explanations for our marriage . . . But all of them are wrong. My love for you is beyond the comprehension of people around us. It has such depth and spiritual beauty that I am sure you are not completely aware of it, as I am only beginning to realize it myself.

My mother, I must say, was never anywhere close to as effusive in her replies. But her letters were just as frequent and long. And although they were mostly long on details about her life, and mine, they were rarely short on affection.

"Kitt and I will be home in about a month and I cannot wait to see you at the airport," she wrote to him from London in October of 1962. ". . . No matter what has happened between us, I feel very close and warm towards you and want it to remain that way. We have a wonderful little family now, and I love it." (Definitely not as mushy as his letters were, but sweet nonetheless.)

A month later, she was evidently still in London, and still longing to see him.

"I have been missing you something awful these past few days and will certainly appreciate the moments I will be with you when I am home," she wrote early that November, shortly before I turned one.

Then there were the letters that she sent him from the Plaza Hotel in New York in April of 1963, in which you can clearly hear her fatigue from being on the road so much: "I want to be home from now on. I don't want this nightclub business anymore. I want to concentrate more on acting, do the dance school at home, live simply, and be much happier. I hate nightclubs, no matter how successful I may be in them . . ."

This was followed by yet another that concluded: "We love you very much . . . at least I do . . . baby Kitt is too young for me to make that statement . . ." It concludes, "Love you . . . love you . . . love you . . . love you . . . love you. . . ."

So maybe she actually had loved him at one point.

Another letter from him talks about how she is going to be gone for three months, and he doesn't know how he's going to survive it. Three months *is* a long time to leave a husband. But she was the breadwinner in the family, with a very successful career. It was a level of success she had worked hard to attain. She often performed overseas because those engagements were easier for her to get, in large part because issues of race were less pronounced over there. So traveling was always a part of the game.

Of course, this was long before technology like Skype, Zoom, and FaceTime ever existed, let alone the ease of email. Or fax machines, for that matter. If only they'd had cellphones, they might have remained married much longer. But long-distance phone calls were complicated to make, and international "snail mail" was slow and unreliable at best. Even though they appear to have written to each other almost daily when they were apart, those letters must have taken a long, long time to arrive.

And that began to take its toll.

"There was another mail delivery today and nothing from you," my father once wrote to her. "I am beginning to get worried. There must be something very wrong with you, for you not to have

written by now. I wish I knew how to find out if you are all right."
Countless other letters share similar frustrations, which eventually
led to things between them falling completely apart.

My mother had soon built an enormous reservoir of hostility
toward my father. They had known from the start, and presumably
both accepted, that my mother was going to be the main breadwinner between them. But soon after I was born, I think she had
already begun to get the first inklings that this was not going to be
the dream marriage she had hoped for.

And my mother was very much someone for whom, if you
hurt her, that was it. You weren't getting a second chance. It was a
defense mechanism that she needed to protect herself.

She may have been disappointed in him, not just as a husband but also a father. I was the center of her universe, and she
wanted him to feel the same way about me. Not that he ever
really had the opportunity to show that. Granted, this was back in
the early '60s. Fathers weren't nearly as involved with their children
as they are today. But it still couldn't have been easy for him. From
the moment that I was born, my mother kept me by her side, never
wanting to be far from my sight. Or me from hers. I was really the
first blood-related "family" she had ever known. And she was (and
remained) completely devoted to me. She was always "A Mother
First." After my birth, everything else became secondary.

Including, or maybe especially, my father.

Many other factors, of course, contributed to the growing rift
between them. Chief among them were my father's drug addiction
and the growing distrust that my mother felt toward him, mostly

about financial matters. She had purchased two buildings in New York City, back in 1959 or 1960, on Fifth Avenue and 92nd Street, and for the rest of her life she remained convinced that he had sold them without her permission while she was away on tour. I don't know what the truth is. I only know that she didn't have them anymore. And that my mother would lament, well into her seventies, "If only I still had those townhouses. . . ." She believed he had sold them to pay off some sort of drug debt that he had incurred.

Was he guilty of financial shenanigans? Who knows? He probably did sell those buildings to pay off some sort of debt. Whether or not it had anything to do with drugs, I have no idea. A lot of things that my father did weren't exactly kosher. His family had been quite well off, and when my grandmother died, all of the grandchildren were left money. My mother always said that my father had emptied my trust fund. I like to think better of people, but when I was an adult, I learned that this was true and he actually had spent all the money my grandmother had left me.

But the biggest cause of the demise of their marriage was probably my mother's constant traveling for work. Their letters often expressed hopes that they would soon be together more often. My mother alluded to her determination to give up touring and spend more time at home. But that was never to be. By the time they split for good, there was an emotional chasm between them wider than any ocean that had ever kept them apart.

At that point, I was still too young to remember their ever having expressed anything but antagonism toward one another.

But I know now, from reading their early correspondence, that their relationship sure didn't start out that way.

Take this 1960 letter from my father, which talked about the spiritual nature of his love. It went on to gush almost poetically about the extraordinary depth—or should I say height?—of his feelings.

It brings to my mind a thought that I had about ten years ago, when I was in the Sequoia National Forest in Northern Calif. I had run away from home and was looking for work in a logging camp. I was riding on a bus looking at those beautiful, majestic trees. I was very lonely. And I thought that I hope someday that I would find a mate for me that I would love so much that it would bring out the strength and spiritual feeling that I felt from looking at those beautiful trees that nature had created. The feeling that these trees would last forever as I want my love for you to last. Forever.

Forever? Not quite. By the time I turned two, my parents had already separated. They were divorced on March 26, 1964, before I was even 3.

Interestingly enough, it was my mother who kept all this correspondence between them. Although she never brought any of these letters to my attention while she was alive, I find it fascinating, and telling, that there was something about the words these pages contain that was important enough for her to treasure.

CHAPTER 9

Second Thoughts

What I do today is how I am interpreted tomorrow.

Yet another disappointment. One more man who had let her down. So our growing family never grew further.

My mother said at times that she had wanted to have a second child. Many of her letters to my father refer to that desire. But they also reveal that she had a variety of thoughts about the issue, and some of them were *second* thoughts.

"Now I would like to have another," she wrote to my father in late 1962, when I was still an infant. "The only thing is I hate going through the getting out of shape and all, now that I have my figure back. But I think it would be worth it to have them close together. Then, too, when I think of having another and it doesn't turn out to be anything like baby Kitt . . ."

Obviously, I think it was a case of everything working out the way it's supposed to be. It certainly would have been harder for her to hit the road with two children in tow. And what if the second child had been a boy? That poor kid! Not quite sure how my mother would have handled that, since she really didn't know what to do with boys.

I used to ask her sometimes, "What would you have named a second child?" Having her name carried on was so important to her that "Kitt" was the only choice my parents had ever selected.

After we found out that George Foreman had named all five of his sons George, we would often joke about it. She would say, "Well, I guess I would have just had Kitt One and Kitt Two."

Nooooo! That would have been like Thing One and Thing Two from *The Cat in the Hat!* Obviously, she was just kidding. Then again, I don't even have a middle name. So it's probably a good thing that she only had one child.

My father, though, did have another child, a son from his second marriage. His name was Chad, and he was eight years younger than I was. My father remarried—twice, actually—after my parents divorced. First, to a Filipino woman named Jan. My mother really liked her. She was a beautiful, diminutive woman. She radiated kindness. But there must have been some painful things going on inside her, for she suddenly committed suicide when Chad was only two years old.

After Jan killed herself, my mother was really angry at my father. She had been able to remove herself from the marriage and take her child with her. She was heartbroken that Jan hadn't been able to find that strength. Obviously, my mother's financial independence had helped make that transition an easier one. The most heartbreaking thing, though, was that when Jan died, she left this little boy in my father's hands.

After that, my mother desperately wanted to get custody of Chad. She felt that he would have been much better off living with us. But there was no way any court was going to allow that. He wasn't my mother's biological child. Besides, my father would never have let that happen. His attitude was, "You got my daughter. I am not going to give you my son!"

But as unstable as a celebrity life can be, the truth is that the everyday existence my mother gave me was actually very stable. She didn't lead a wild, crazy, party life. Far from it! My mother went to work, and then she came home. And when she was home, she was a mom. Always a mom first. And when she was on the road working, I was often right there with her. She was never comfortable being away from me, so her going to work meant my staying in either the apartment or a hotel room nearby, with my nanny or housekeeper, and my mother going to the theater, doing her work, and then coming straight back to me.

For that reason, my mother felt that Chad would have been much better off with us. At that point in his life, my father was not a stable person, or so she felt. His drug addiction had significantly escalated over the years. People often told my mother that they would go to my father's house and find drug paraphernalia lying around. She felt helpless that there was this little boy running around in diapers or toddler clothes, surrounded by drugs and strangers.

That's why my mother tried to convince my father to give her custody of Chad. But that was never going to happen.

So Chad grew up in my father's house without a mother. Then, many years later, after my father had died, Chad suddenly died under mysterious circumstances. His friends told me that he had come down with the flu. He went to the hospital one day, and the next thing they knew he had gone into cardiac arrest and died. He was only in his late thirties at the time. What really happened remains a mystery to me.

Even before that, Chad had never been healthy. My father used to say that he had lupus, or some other type of autoimmune disease, and various other health issues. When he died, he was pretty much alone in the world. He never did have many friends. He was a loner, much like our father was. He was also very attached to my father, just as much as I was attached to my mother, if not more so. I think that my father caused Chad's dependence upon him, and then, as my father got older, his own health was also quite poor. His injuries from the war and living a rough life eventually caused many health issues, particularly toward the end. So Chad was the one who took care of him.

When I was young, I was often angry that my mother had felt the need to protect me from my father. I knew that children are supposed to have two parents, not just one. They're supposed to have the yin and the yang. I had only had my mother. Yes, I had all of her, and as I got older, I realized how blessed I really was. But as a little girl, there had been no buffer. And as an only child, there was no one to turn to when you sometimes wanted to throw everything in the room at the parent standing before you. There was no one else I could go to and scream, "Can you believe what Mom just did?"

My mother was the only outlet I had. As I got older, I realized that my mother had been right. (Don't you just hate admitting that?) My father wasn't the most ethical person in the world. And the truth is that I had so many mixed feelings of my own that time spent with my father didn't always go smoothly.

When I was young, she encouraged the relationship and would often make plans for us. But I didn't like going to my father's house. It was creepy. He had this weird house that overlooked the city of Los Angeles. The house itself was big, but he lived like a bachelor, and I remember thinking it felt kind of seedy. Yet my mother encouraged me to spend some weekends there anyway, because she thought it was important.

My mother also fought my father for years for child support. Not because she needed his money. Quite the opposite. "It has nothing to do with the money," she said. That, in fact, was my father's argument. "You don't need the money, so why are you coming after me for it?" But it was her firm belief that if you are financially invested in something, or someone, then you are likely to take more interest. All this ever got her, though, was more frustration and more pushback from him.

As a young girl, I blamed my mother for keeping my father away from me. But as I got older, I realized that this wasn't the case at all. She hadn't been keeping us apart. Rather, in her own way, she had been protecting me from being hurt, because he hadn't really been seeking me out to have a true father-daughter relationship.

That being said, my mother wasn't exactly always the easiest person to deal with, either. So, on my father's side of the aisle, it probably seemed like, "It's just much easier not to have anything to do with her." Not with me, but with her. It was easier if he just let me be with my mother and not be a part of our lives.

My mother had a house in London, though, and for a time my father also rented a house there as well, surprisingly. So I spent a little time with him there. But as I got older, I rarely saw him at all, and by the time I was an adult I had almost no relationship with him whatsoever. In fact, he never even met my children. When he died, I hadn't seen him since long before my son had been born.

So when I learned that he had died, I had very little emotion about it. Any sadness I felt was for the little girl who had yearned to have a "Daddy." Because I believe family is something that you work at. Relationships are something you work at. Even if you are born to someone, if you don't have a relationship with them, then it's hard to feel a connection.

But I think I had anger toward both my parents. They both played a role here. My mother was angry at my father for not being trustworthy. He was yet another man who had disappointed her.

My father, meanwhile, had his own demons. Along with his wounds from the war, he had psychological wounds from childhood.

He had a mother who was incredibly controlling and strong. Probably one of the very reasons my mother loved her so much.

My grandmother, as she often said herself, had never really liked the fact that she had given birth to a boy. She had never wanted a boy. She remained angry about it, and, sadly, that's how she treated him from the day he was born.

When my mother went to the hospital to give birth to me, my grandmother actually said to her, "If you don't have a girl, I'll never speak to you again." Wow! Good thing she got her wish, right? My father suffered for being a son. My grandmother also had three girls, one of whom was a tomboy as a child, and had it even worse than my father. Her other two daughters were her pride and joy.

So, when my father chose to marry my mother—this strong, independent, and successful woman—my grandmother was thrilled. Not necessarily because my mother was famous. She just thought that my mother was simply the greatest! Later, when their marriage fell apart, my grandmother only fueled the fire between them.

"I could have warned you of this, Kitty," she said. (Most people who knew my mother well called her Kitty.) "This is exactly what I expected of him. It doesn't surprise me at all."

When my parents divorced, my father's entire family sided with my mother, including, or maybe especially, his own mother, the true matriarch of the family. He was "odd man out" bigtime, and he had to deal with that.

See, we all have family dramas. There's no such thing as The Perfect Family.

On top of that, my father had to deal with the fact that he didn't get to bond with me the way a parent normally bonds with a child. From practically the moment I was born, my mother took me away on the road. And even though she was always writing from different locations, describing to him what I was like, and the powerful love she had for me, he had no way of experiencing that himself.

"I can't wait till you get to know her," she wrote to him, but he never got that opportunity. Just as her life on the road didn't lend itself to having a normal marriage, it didn't allow for a normal family life, either. We were all deprived of that. And remember her writing about how I completed her? Most of the time, it really was just the two of us. It would have been hard for my father to fit into that, even if he'd been the greatest guy in the world. In some ways, it was the perfect storm.

CHAPTER 10

Our Race—The Human One

Just because you are different
doesn't mean you have to be rejected.

There used to be a law in the South known as the one-drop rule. It maintained that if you had even one ancestor with Black heritage—"one drop of Black blood" was the expression—then you were considered to be Black yourself. I find that interesting because, pardon the pun, it's so black and white. Two columns. To be seen as completely separate. Defined by a rule created to maintain this distance.

The problem is . . . well, there are just so many problems with this rule, I'm not even sure how one begins to tackle it.

For my mother, racial identity was just a silly construct. A man-made concept that segregates people, based solely on the color of their skin. "I don't carry myself as a black person but as a woman that belongs to everybody," she told *The Washington Post* in 2005. "After all, it's the general public that made me—not any one particular group. So I don't think of myself as belonging to any particular group and never have."

Neither have I. Why *do* we all need to be classified as belonging to one group?

In that regard, I often think about Barack Obama. He made history by becoming the first Black president of the United States. But only his father was Black. His mother was white. He was just as much white as he was Black. Why isn't he just as easily considered white? My mother was Black and my father was white, and many people say that I'm clearly white. Just because of the way I look. How does that make any sense? There are even people who deny my very existence, simply because I don't have the features or the "coloring" that they think I should have.

I know exactly who both of my parents were. Yet some people continue to question my ancestry all the time. They openly say to me on social media, "There is no way you could be your mother's biological daughter. She clearly lied to you." Or they simply ask, "Are you adopted?" They don't think that I look anything like my mother, since I am so much lighter-skinned than she was and my hair is blonde. For that reason alone, they make an automatic assumption. "You can't be her daughter. You must be adopted."

"Nope. Not adopted!" I say.

With the rise of the Black Lives Matter movement, this has become a hot topic. People don't just wonder anymore. They openly attack me. I get this almost every day.

Here's one response I have: "On what planet do you think a Black woman could have adopted a white baby in 1961? Or for that matter, that could happen even today?"

Then there are the people who insist that I must have had plastic surgery in order to look more Caucasian and "pass" as white. As if I would ever do that, or that I feel a need to identify myself as part of any one specific group.

Why do they think I want or need that? If we all had genetic testing, it would reveal the extent to which most of us are all mixed up. We're blended. Wasn't this country originally created as a melting pot? Well, you know what, guys? We succeeded. We're a melting pot! Let's embrace that.

It amazes me that because I don't look the way many people think I should look, they question my identity. That's mind-boggling to me. I get comments like this on my website, SimplyEartha.com, almost every day. Most of the time, I simply ignore them.

On the one hand, I hesitate to dignify them with an answer. On the other, though, I think we need to keep that conversation going because the stereotypes of how we think each other should look are contributing to the rifts within society—the anger and the battles that we are experiencing right now.

I'm referring to battles about race with which my mother was all too familiar.

"I'm not black and I'm not white and I'm not pink and I'm not green," she once said. "Eartha Kitt has no color, and that is how barriers are broken."

Unfortunately, those barriers persist to this day and still need to be broken.

When people used to question my identity, I mostly thought it was funny. I knew that I wasn't adopted. I have photographs of my mother being wheeled out of Cedars of Lebanon Hospital in 1961 beaming as she cradles me, her newborn baby, in her arms. Do people actually imagine that my mother had those staged? That this was some sort of conspiracy? How absurd! So it never really bothered me when people said those things. I guess my mother raised me to understand that sometimes people just say things.

The truth is, though, that I actually do look a lot like my mother. People may be thrown by the coloring, but my facial structure is a lot like hers. Also, my mother had these beauty marks on her body, and I also have beauty marks in the exact same spots. One on my left shoulder, and another on my back, right below my left shoulder blade. That was how, as a little girl, I identified myself as her daughter. "I know I'm yours because we have the same beauty marks!" I would say.

I also remember seeing those questionnaires on which you would be asked to check off your race. These days, they give you lots of choices, including ones that reflect mixed race. But when I was young, they didn't have a lot of options. So there were times when I would check off all of them. Or sometimes I would check off none of them.

My mother brought me up to believe that the whole thing was just silly. That's why I would simply check off everything—white, Black, Hispanic, Asian, Native American, and whatever else there might be. Why not? It was such a stupid question to begin with. Why wasn't "human" on there? Why not really confuse them?

In many ways, I was also a little rebel. My mother raised me to be a little version of herself. So I would rebel in my own little way. She taught me that the issue didn't make any sense. It was just a foolish expectation that society had—this need to pinpoint everyone's race. My father was as lily-white as you could get. I mean literally! His skin was pale and pasty white, like the color of the ghost-white walls in my living room. He was Irish and German. His family couldn't have gotten any whiter.

As for my mother? She didn't know who her father was, so we only had her mother to go by, and the few family members my mother had met over the years. She did have half-sisters, and they were significantly darker than my mother was. My mother didn't actually know *for sure* that her father had been white. She and everyone else simply assumed it. Assumed she was of mixed race, and that half of that mix was white.

Everyone is always talking on social media these days about how you identify yourself race-wise. It's as if people have this need to know. *Why* do they need to know? People often message me from the area in South Carolina where my mother grew up. "You need to find your roots," they say. "You need to connect with your family, and your people." And I think, "Why do I need to do that?"

But I think it's really interesting. The more we find out about our genetic makeup, the more we realize how mixed up we really are in terms of racial makeup. And that brings me back to the subject of how you identify yourself—who you believe you are. And how weird it was that my mother didn't know who or what she was because she didn't know who her father was. That had to be a very strange feeling.

My mother took great pride in being able to snub the way that society functions. It infuriated her that as a Black person in the entertainment business, you had to be categorized as either a Gospel singer or a jazz singer or a blues singer. You couldn't just be a *singer.*

Because she had a unique sound, record companies would ask, "What *are* you?" Again, she wasn't quite dark enough to be really Black, and not light enough to be white, which left executives stumped. "Is she Black?" they would say. "Is she Indian? What *is* she? We have to have a category."

When my mother started as a recording artist at RCA, she had just returned from France after becoming famous there, and she had a unique sound. She had an unidentifiable accent that wasn't American. She also had a look that was exotic. Yet she was from South Carolina. Add to these things that she spoke several languages. She sang a song in Turkish, and she sang songs in French. The record company was perplexed about how to classify her.

"What do you do with an American who sings in different languages?" they said. "Or a Black woman who is feline, sultry, and exotic?"

Back then, it was different than it is today. You couldn't really forge your own path. Entertainers these days are allowed to cross over a lot more. Blurring the genre lines is easier than it was when my mother started out. Now you have platforms like Spotify, YouTube, iTunes, Netflix, Amazon Prime, and HBO, where you find actors, singers, and musicians from all genres, sometimes appearing in unexpected projects.

Having successfully battled stereotyping, my mother found great joy in having given birth to a human being who was even harder to categorize than she was. Now she could say about me, "Go ahead and try to pinpoint her. Try to put her in a box."

When she would tell me that I was a walking United Nations, I think the ultimate message she was giving me was, "You can't be held down. You can't be held back. You are anything and everything you want to be."

These were lessons that she imparted to me before I could even speak. And she expressed them with incredible pride, joy, and authenticity. The attitude she conveyed was that being unique was a great thing. Being "different" wasn't something to hide. The message I heard was, "Walk around like a peacock, with your chest held high, because you are everything to everybody! And you belong everywhere you want to be!"

How incredibly empowering is that for a mother to give to her daughter?

When I was little, she would read to me every night, and one of our favorite books was *The Sneetches and Other Stories*. The title story provided a wonderful example of acceptance. I can understand why my mother loved it so much.

Among all the Dr. Seuss stories, she chose this book over the more typical ones like *The Cat in the Hat* and *Green Eggs and Ham* because of its powerful moral lesson. It was about equality.

The Sneetches were these yellow bird-like creatures who lived on the beaches. Some had green stars on their bellies. The rest had none. The star-bellied Sneetches felt that they were better than the plain-bellied Sneetches. One day, though, a character named Sylvester McMonkey McBean came along. He got the plain-bellied Sneetches to pay him to go into his Star-On machine and get stars on their bellies, too.

Then the star-bellied Sneetches began to say, "Now we need to have *no* stars on our bellies." So they paid him to go into his Star-Off machine to take their stars *off.* This process went around and around, so that by the time Sylvester McMonkey McBean drove away, the Sneetches didn't know who was who anymore. (Believe me, Dr. Seuss does a much better job of telling the story than I just did, so I recommend reading it yourself and to your own children . . . or to somebody else's, with their permission.)

The moral of the story, of course, is about diversity and tolerance. After wasting a lot of money and energy, they finally learned to live all together. It didn't matter whether they had stars on their bellies or not.

The whole concept of treating people differently because of the color of their skin was incomprehensible to my mother. Unfortunately, it's nothing new, and progress is slow. If my mother were still with us, then she would probably look at all of the racial issues going on right now, and the continued racial inequality, and say, "The more things change, the more they stay the same."

Had she been here to witness the horrible actions that led to the deaths of George Floyd and Breonna Taylor, among others, I know my mother would have been deeply saddened and dismayed. I doubt she would have been shocked, though. After all, this kind of behavior has been going on in our country for a very, very long time.

Personally, other than that one episode in South Africa, I rarely saw my mother treated differently because of her race. Most people, even if they were racist, were more impressed with her fame than they were worried about her race. Yes, there were a few incidents in which she answered the door and a delivery person assumed she was the maid. But in our everyday lives, almost everybody knew that my mother was a celebrity.

That, though, had not always been the case. She once wrote about a night in 1952, early in her career, when she was performing at a nightclub in London and she passed a table of distinguished-looking men whose conversation she overheard:

"'She is beautiful.'

"'I wonder what nationality she is!'

"'She must be from Indonesia.'"

Then one man said, "Ah, she's nothing but a n———.'"

She was so hurt by this that she was unable to finish her show. But I almost never witnessed her being treated differently or ostracized by anyone.

Then again, by the time I was six, my mother was playing Catwoman on *Batman,* which was a really big deal. To see a woman of color dressed in a skintight bodysuit, cast opposite a white man, with palpable sexual tension between them? That was unprecedented in 1967. And a bold move to undertake by all parties involved, I might add.

Television thrusts even the most famous of entertainers to a new and different level of fame. People would recognize my mother on the street and ask her to purr for them (a uniquely feline sound that my mother possessed, and which soon became almost synonymous with the character of Catwoman). She was accepted by everyone, as far as I could see.

Yet only a decade earlier, in 1957, I believe, my mother had once seen a white man who appeared to be having a heart attack in an elevator in Texas. She went to his side to help him and was promptly arrested due to the strict Jim Crow laws there, mandating racial segregation at the time. She was already famous at this point, but she was still put in jail. Only then did they ask her name. "You didn't bother to ask my name before you arrested me," she told them. "You didn't seem to care who or what I was." Once she identified herself, apologies were made. But the deed was already done.

When the current generation of young people see atrocities like the death of George Floyd on the news, they're stunned. But somebody my mother's age would say, "How is that so much different from what happened in the '50s and '60s, and for eons before that?" It remains horrific, especially considering that it is founded on a falsehood. How much melanin we have in our skin has nothing to do with who we are as human beings, the level of our intelligence, or what is in our minds and hearts and souls.

And my mother would be among the first to say that.

So she might not be surprised by the latest incidents, but she would also not be dissuaded from continuing to keep these important conversations going—anything to show the ridiculousness of treating people differently because of the color of their skin.

Would she actually be marching in the streets proclaiming "Black Lives Matter?" Probably. Even though she was terrified of large crowds. As a heart-felt supporter of Dr. Martin Luther King Jr., she believed passionately in racial equality, as well as in the freedom to protest peacefully.

In 2016, quarterback Colin Kaepernick took a knee during "The Star-Spangled Banner" to protest racial inequality and police brutality against unarmed Black citizens, and he ended up losing his job and his football career. What he represented in that silence has now blown up around us. I admire the strength and conviction that it takes to stand up (or kneel, as in this case) for what you believe in. And I think my mother would have understood the desire to speak out and be heard by protesting quietly and non-violently. I can see her wanting to support that effort and continue it.

And as disheartened as she might be by many recent events, she would not have been deterred from her lifelong need to talk about what it is to be a human being, and the need to demonstrate kindness and empathy toward one another.

My mother believed that society cannot function properly without empathy. Regardless of our race—or ethnicity, political persuasion, religion, sexuality, or any other factor—we have to be able to see each other as human beings, first and foremost, and not as enemies. We need to understand that we are all on this planet together, and that we are all entitled to take up the space that we occupy and live our lives however we choose.

My mother loved the art of conversation and the exchange of ideas, and she encouraged people to listen to each other. That doesn't mean that we have to agree with, or even like, what the other person has to say. It's just essential that we stop and listen.

So, if the way I look helps stimulate that discussion—because one person says, "She looks exactly like her mother," and another says, "She couldn't possibly be her mother's daughter," then at least that is a way to start a dialogue about diversity. It helps to begin an important conversation and bring people to the table.

My mother would approve.

CHAPTER 11

Born to Run

There's no such thing as too much love or too many hugs.

So, as you can see, I was born. Born to run. No, make that fly. From the moment the doctor said I could get on a plane, my mother and I took flight.

She took me with her wherever she went to perform and, as she was internationally famous, that meant that we traveled to places near and far—New York, Great Britain, Sweden, Denmark, Australia, Japan. . . . You name it, I've probably been there.

Even though we were often away for months at a time, my father stayed behind in Beverly Hills, holding down the fort and overseeing my mother's businesses as her CPA. Meanwhile, I served as my mother's constant companion, giving her the roots for which she had always yearned.

"When I think of not having her all these years, I wonder how I managed without her," she wrote to my father in 1962, when I was 10 months old. "She keeps me going."

It wasn't just her imagination. I was somehow attuned to her every need. I was a savvy little girl. Savvy, at least, when it came to my mother. That's where my "savvy" was.

I knew how much she needed me. Needed me to give her whatever stability, or family, she hadn't had growing up. Giving birth to me had provided her with a sense of purpose different from anything else that she had ever had in her life. It was the one thing above all else that she had felt was truly missing.

"I only feel human completely when she is near," she wrote about me in another letter. "Nothing has made me feel more real and alive than she has . . . She is the nicest person I have ever met. She is very considerate, lovable, sensitive, and affectionate." In these feelings, expressed when I was still only a toddler, her desire to fill that void rang out loud and clear.

On a very deep level, I believe I understood that. Even as an infant, I sensed the importance of this role that I believe I was meant to play. My mother felt that I was all that was left. I was a true foundation that she could rely on and trust. This baby girl that she had birthed gave her unconditional love and devotion.

I was everything that she had ever dreamed of. Or maybe I was beyond her dreams. She talked in her letters about how even as an infant I was completely in sync with her in every way. "This baby is so sensitive, even to my moods," she wrote. "She adjusts, and when she feels I am not in a good mood, I think she tries to make me happy. She can cuddle up with an expression that, no matter what kind of mood I was in, I would have to become cheerful."

She had wanted a child more than anything, and as she got older, she claimed that having a baby had been her entire reason for getting married. I was all that she had, and I soon became all that she wanted me to be. I had been born with the exact personality my mother needed. And I grew to adapt to and understand that importance, often sharing with her how I felt that, somehow, God had known I would be the perfect fit for her, answering whatever prayers she may have sent out.

There is a high price that comes with being the most important thing in your mother's life, though. I'm not complaining about it, mind you. I'm just pointing out that, emotionally, there was a toll that went along with that. As a teenager, I felt guilty about spreading my wings and wanting to spend time with my friends. And as a mother myself now, I fully comprehend that children should not be expected to conform to a parent's moods or expectations. Children, and teens especially, often express themselves through separation and even anger, learning by pushing the boundaries set by their parents as they struggle to find their own voices and independence. There were times, as I got older, when my mother took my desire to be separate from her personally, and that wasn't easy—for either of us.

But that part came later. For my mother, being a mother came first, so from the time I was born I was always with her. She didn't want anyone else taking care of me or tending to my needs. She didn't even trust other family members to watch me for long. Even though my paternal grandmother and aunt often accompanied us on tour, my mother made sure that she knew about everything I did, from each morsel of food that went into my mouth to every word that was spoken to me.

And I got a lot *from* her in return. I'm talking about the amount of love I got. She didn't just love me. She *adored* me. She *showed* me love. She would almost smother me with kisses and affection. She was a cuddler and a snuggler. And I was the center of her universe.

What my mother hadn't received as a child, she was damn sure she was going to give as a parent. And so she gave me her love . . . in spades!

I got all that good karma. All the stuff that nourishes you. All of those positive things that strengthen you emotionally, filling you with confidence and self-worth. My mother understood the nurturing power of love. I guess you really comprehend that power when you have been deprived of it.

Children also need some sense of routine and consistency. Those things were not always easy to achieve while traveling the world, though, so my mother would try to maintain a sense of normalcy by creating daily rituals. Bedtime and playtime, in particular, were moments she always carved out in her day, no matter where we were.

Even when she had a performance, getting me ready for bed was a priority, a time when the door was closed and the rest of the world was cut off. This allowed her to focus solely on me and whatever stories I had to tell from my day. During that time, we would read storybooks and sometimes do fun tongue-twister exercises. But mostly we laughed. A lot! My mother taught me that laughter is one of life's most important gifts.

My mother often performed in Copenhagen, and there was a song, based on a Scandinavian nursery rhyme, that she would sing to me called *"Rida, Rida Ranka."* I don't know what it meant, other than that it was about riding a rocking horse, but it began:

Rida, rida ranka,
Hästen heter Blanka . . .

As she sang, she would lie on the floor with her knees in a tucked position, with her legs parallel to the floor. I would sit on her legs with my legs wrapped underneath hers, and she would rock back and forth like a rocking chair, slowly picking up speed so that I would have to hold on tight to not fall off. I'm not sure what I found so funny about this routine, but it was usually impossible for me to stay on her legs, since I would be giggling so hard. I usually ended up rolling on the floor, laughing hysterically.

Eventually, I got too tall to do it anymore. But she would still give it a try, telling me I had to wrap my long, lanky legs even tighter to hold on. I continued to ask her to do this up until I was a teenager. To me, it was better than any amusement park ride.

And when I had friends over, of course they would want to do it, too. My mother was quite athletic and strong, and she got a big kick out of seeing us all get so much enjoyment out of it, along with getting quite a workout.

My mother was very warm and affectionate toward my girl-friends while I was growing up. She loved my friends. And she loved horsing around with them. She'd roll on the floor and wrestle with us, fun things I didn't see any of the other parents doing back then. She would crawl around and act silly, or play animals, or jungle, or whatever else we wanted to do. She enjoyed watching how creative children can be using only their imaginations.

As a child, my mother had needed to rely on her own imagination to help her escape the grim reality of her surroundings, and she embraced and encouraged that in herself, often stating in interviews, "I like to use the freedom of my own imagination."

She would tell me how she had escaped to the outdoors and into the woods and watched nature unfold when she was a child. You could learn a lot, she would say, just through observation. Nature, she found, was fascinating. And not only the obvious parts of Nature, like farm animals and foliage. My mother liked to observe the small workings of the universe.

You don't carry the name Eartha without understanding the earth, I guess.

Ants, and ant colonies, intrigued her. I suppose she had seen a lot of ants in the South. One of the most interesting things about them, to her, was that they all work together, and they don't discriminate against each other. Every ant in the colony pulls its own weight. Yes, there was a queen. (I actually think she liked that part the best—that the colony was ruled by a queen, and they all listened to her.) But my mother would talk about how nobody slacked off in an ant colony. Have you ever seen an ant just "hangin' out?" Nope. That's why I think she was enamored of them. Ants are constantly busy. Moving. Working. And that's what my mother was like, too.

She didn't know what to do with herself if she wasn't working.

If she didn't have an engagement, and she was home, you would most likely find her in the garden, working. There was always work to be done.

That was really important to my mother. She always needed to be productive, making something, or getting stuff done.

If you had down time and you were just sitting around doing nothing? Well, that was unacceptable to her.

Tending to her garden would lead to her cooking up what she had picked, of course, which in turn led to sharing those dishes with friends and/or cast members.

When there were breaks at work, she could usually be found doing needlepoint. "I couldn't just sit backstage, or in my dressing room or on a movie set, and do nothing," she would say. "There's so much down time. I had to keep busy doing *something*."

That's why we have needlepoint "everything" now, from carpets to cushions to wall hangings. Everything was a potential needlepoint project to my mother. And, as with everything else that she did, she loved sharing her creations.

I'm not as big a fan of needlepoint. She would often say to me, "I made this needlepoint pillow for you." Or sometimes it was a rug.

"I don't want it," I would reply. But that never did dissuade her from making another masterpiece. I still have a lot of needle-pointed creations in storage.

My mother and I were like two pieces of a puzzle that fit together perfectly. The irony was how different we looked.

When my father was peering through the hospital nursery window right after I was born, a woman standing nearby asked him which one was Eartha Kitt's baby. It was all over the papers that I had been born. This woman, a fan of my mother's, wanted to get a look for herself. So my father pointed to me.

"No, it can't be *that* baby," she replied. "That's a little *white* baby."

Little did she realize that the man she was talking to was the father. My mother laughed when she heard this story. She thought it was hysterical. She and my father were on the same page about at least one thing: They loved that I had all of my mother's features, but I had his coloring, blonde hair, and light-colored eyes. I was a real mix of the two of them. They both loved to upset the applecart.

CHAPTER 12

No Ums, Uhs, or "Likes"

*Spoil a child today and tomorrow you may
have headaches and heartaches galore.*

I may have helped them upset the applecart, but bad behavior was not a trait I would ever have been allowed to exhibit. My mother never allowed me to act like a spoiled brat. Manners were a requirement, yes, but treating people with respect was even more important. She was very conscious about privileged children (and adults, for that matter) acting like they were entitled. Her international fame meant that she performed for actual royalty at times and, sometimes, interacted with their children. My mother despised it when these youngsters were impolite, or didn't behave with courtesy and kindness. That was something for which she had zero tolerance. So she certainly wasn't going to raise her own child to believe that was OK.

I remember going to a birthday party once for a little boy who was the prince of some small country, but I don't remember where. This little boy didn't say hello to my mother when we arrived and was very rude. And my mother called him on it.

"Excuse me, young man!" she said. "You do not speak to me in that manner. I don't care what princedom you come from!" A person's "station" or status in life was no excuse for nastiness.

But her being strict and demanding about behavior and manners only served me well. No question! The best compliment I could possibly receive was to be told "how nice I was." Once, when I was a teenager, there was a woman I met while on the road with my mother who commented that she was surprised by how "down to earth and kind" I was. I still remember how much pride I felt upon hearing her words! My behavior, as I had been taught, was all that I could really control in life, and so how I treated others, and the impact that had, was of utmost importance. My mother instilled in me the necessity to have respect for everyTHING and everyBODY.

Her strictness, I feel, was a huge gift. That becomes particularly clear when I see how people tend to treat one another. First of all, I think children yearn for structure. Structure, obviously, is an essential part of society. That's why traffic rules work, for the most part. Without them, we'd be crashing into each other all the time and have utter chaos in the streets. (Yes, there are places where, even with rules in place, pandemonium ensues, but I think that makes my case.)

Having good manners may sound trite and petty, but it isn't at all. Being polite is not just about common courtesy. It's kindness. It's empathy. It's being present, and understanding that we all need to be mindful of each other's existence. Understanding that our own behavior affects other people, which in turn ripples out to many more. So take a beat, and sometimes maybe even bite your tongue, smile, and BE KIND.

As my mother would say, there are times when you may not want to be polite, and you may not even want to be kind. But having the discipline to be that way anyway is just common decency. And that is something that many people appear to have lost.

Poor diction was another one of my mother's pet peeves. It made her crazy that many people—especially young people—would constantly pepper their sentences with "Um . . . uh . . . ya know . . . like . . ." So, into our evening bedtime ritual, she often incorporated mind exercises. Before I would go to sleep, we would sit on my bed and, beginning with one corner, I would have to name everything I saw around the room without once saying "um," "uh," "ya know," or "like." Not as easy as it sounds, by the way. Little did I realize it at the time, but my mother was teaching me to think quickly, and to use proper language, too.

For example, I might say, "The television is hanging on the white wall next to the outlet with the three switches, which has a painting right above it." No, it wasn't poetry, or worthy of a song lyric, but it would be a description of all the things that I saw in detail with little hesitation or resorting to any of those little connector words or other so-called speech disfluencies.

Pronouncing words clearly and eloquently was similarly imperative to my mother. When you enunciate, she felt, it not only helps people understand what you're saying, but also encourages them to pay attention and show you a greater level of respect.

Coming from the South, then growing up in the projects in New York, my mother hadn't had much formal education, but she didn't think that was any excuse for using poor diction. She credited one of her teachers in New York with introducing her to the art of public speaking. I think it was Mrs. Banks, the same woman who had sent her to see José Ferrer perform. She saw something in my mother, an innate curiosity, that she felt could be developed if encouraged, so she assigned her monologues from old English plays to learn. These often-challenging, tricky passages forced her to slow down the pace of her speech, in order to deliver the lines clearly and with confidence. My mother always held teachers in the highest regard due to the impact a couple of them had had on her, an impression that stayed with her until the day she died. This, however, led to her intolerance of others who did not show a desire for self-improvement, often resulting in her frustration at what she deemed laziness when she would hear the English language spoken incorrectly. She felt there was no excuse, for example, for someone to say, "He done 'axed' me that," when referring to someone having asked them a question. She understood from having traveled throughout the world that you were not going to command any respect if you couldn't enunciate or speak properly.

This did lead to her contemporaries sometimes making comments like, "Oh, Kitty, you think you're better than everyone else." Or, "You're just trying to act white!"

Because of the way she spoke, people often assumed that my mother was from a foreign country. She certainly didn't sound like she was from the South. But she *intentionally* didn't sound like she was from the South. It had nothing to do with being anti-South. To her, it was just about speaking clearly.

And that was very important to her because she had grown up feeling that she was decidedly not respected. So this was her way of taking control of that.

The truth is that it was difficult to identify where my mother was from. She was very deliberate about the way she spoke, as well as about her mannerisms and the way that she presented herself. I think she always felt, deep down, that she was a survivor, and from the moment she was removed from the South, she had started to carve out her own path, a path based solely on faith in herself and a willingness to "put in the work" that would allow her to make a mark on this world.

So when it came to parenting, along with all the love and affection that she showered on me, it was equally crucial to her that I be disciplined and well-educated. With all the travel she had done early in her career, my mother believed it was important to learn to speak more than one's own native language. She'd had to learn on her own as she went along, but she decided I was going to be introduced to other languages from a very early age.

Her years growing up in Harlem had taught her Spanish (which she spoke fluently), and her years spent in Paris meant her French was more than decent. So she often spoke Spanish to me in our house, and when it came time to start my formal education, she decided that I should attend a French school. Not a boarding school, though; my going away wasn't even a consideration for my hands-on mother. No, a private school in California, Le Lycée Francais de Los Angeles.

For that reason, I experienced a bit of a different scene than most kids do. It wasn't just that the curriculum was all in French, and that many of the students were from foreign countries, or at least their parents were. There were many "typical" things that I wasn't exposed to.

Don't get me wrong. I loved my school. But I wanted to be cool and hip, and that was hard to do when you are required to wear a uniform! I hated wearing that uniform, which I did from the day that I started kindergarten. I was always jealous when I would see public school kids out looking so much cooler than I felt. (Maybe that's why I not only love fashion now, but eventually chose to buy a women's clothing boutique.)

I so wanted to be like those kids. The kids I saw on TV. The ones hanging out in the schoolyard in their own colorful clothes. Instead, I had to wear a white button-down shirt with a rounded collar and dark blue blazer with a gold crest. Not to mention a skirt. And not just any skirt. A gray pleated skirt. And the length of the skirt had to be measured. It could be no more than one inch above the knee. That felt like torture. Uniform torture. My freedom to use my own imagination by choosing my own daily wardrobe was quashed.

Even the socks we had to wear were preordained. They had to be blue. And the shoes had to be navy. Can you feel my pain!? There were also restrictions on how and when you wore all of these things. You were allowed to take your blazer off, but only at certain times. And when you did, you had to put on a navy sweater instead.

Boys had to wear the same blazer with a white button-down shirt and maroon tie.

Argh. The monotony!

It was all very regimented. And felt very restrictive. And, as well-behaved as I was, I detested that. Way more than once, I was reprimanded and got a mark against me for my skirt being too short, because I would roll the waistband up to make it shorter. I would roll it up to be uber short. Miniskirt short, although I always wore gym shorts underneath, so it's not like you could ever see my underwear. I wasn't *that* risqué. Talk about pushing the limits, right? (I was quite the little rabble-rouser, I bet you're thinking.) And I was usually caught wearing the wrong shoes because I would wear sneakers instead of whatever they were— navy saddle shoes. Oh, and I almost never had my blazer on, and I would unbutton my shirt at the top, or have it only half tucked in, which was also not allowed. (Who knew the half tuck would actually become a thing? I guess I was a fashion influencer and didn't even know it.) That's how the rebel in me came out. (You can stop laughing now.)

You wouldn't catch me smoking cigarettes in the girls' bathroom, or anything like that. I was nowhere near that cool. It's not like I ever did anything that my mother had to be called into the office about. I don't know how much tattling there was to her about my uniform improprieties. But my skirt was often way too short. And I almost always had on the wrong socks.

But no matter what I said, my mother wouldn't let me go to public school. She insisted that I go to the Lycée instead. She just thought that it would provide a better education and environment for me. And, of course, my mother was right. (I know that's a cliché, but it so often turns out that way.)

Every morning, my mother would drop me at school, which was about thirty-five minutes each way from our house. When I was little, she drove a white Cadillac—one of those big Cadillacs with the pointy fins. To be dropped off at school, you would have to drive up a big hill and then join the line of cars as they formed a big loop in front of these large gates, where a few school employees waited to open the car doors for the kids. Then each child would run through the gate, and the parent would make a circle and drive off.

My mother would have a scarf around her head, have no makeup on, and be wearing her workout clothes. That's how she was usually dressed. Very laid-back, as were most people there, even if they were celebrities. This was California, remember. You didn't see people dressed up that much.

Also, Beverly Hills at the time was much more of a small town. It was nothing like the stereotype that we see and hear about on reality shows these days. Back then, Rodeo Drive didn't have the reputation for being overly excessive. And it wasn't. It was always nice, but it didn't have the kind of flashiness you see there now. People who lived in Beverly Hills were financially successful, but they were mostly working people. They were kind of regular folk. Maybe they worked in movie studios or other aspects of the entertainment industry, but they still got up every day and went to work, just like everybody else. Then they went back to their houses, which may have looked grander than the average home, but weren't like they are today.

Now everything there is opulent. I drive through Beverly Hills and it feels so over-the-top. But that's not at all what it was like when I lived there. It was a little town.

I remember going to this one shoe store there. Everyone went to this little store. It was called Harry Harris, and that's where you bought your kids' shoes.

The shoes that I got at Harry Harris when I was growing up weren't ordinary shoes, though. I wore corrective shoes, because I had been born knock-kneed. So I had to wear these uncomfortable and ugly corrective shoes for eight or nine years. They were stiff and white, and sometimes, because they were so boxy looking, my mother would mix up the right shoe with the left, and put the wrong shoe on the wrong foot. Truth is, they were so uncomfortable either way that even I had a difficult time telling when they weren't on correctly.

I remember vividly the time that I went to Harry Harris with my mother, and I was so excited because I was finally going to get a pair of regular Mary Janes. And not just any Mary Janes. White patent leather Mary Janes! (I told you . . . stylin'.)

To me, this was the biggest day of my life because I was going to finally get measured for normal shoes and say goodbye to those torture-chamber, hideous-looking, corrective shoes. I couldn't wait to step onto that metal foot-measuring thing, find my dream shoes, and get a balloon. This was the kind of small store in which everybody knew you by name. And you knew everybody there by name. It was welcoming and safe.

The day that we went to Harry Harris to get my first pair of non-corrective shoes, I walked out thinking I was the coolest thing ever, because I finally had shoes like the ones everybody else wore. No kid wants to be noticed for wearing ugly and uncomfortable footwear.

Until then, starting from when I was a baby, my mother had spent most evenings massaging my legs. My knock-kneed little legs. Having been trained as a dancer, she believed that muscle memory was important. And that if she did this consistently, night after night, she could get the muscles to start to "think" differently by training them to go in a different direction. So she started these exercises early, on my still-malleable limbs.

When I got old enough, she also enrolled me in ballet classes, because she felt that if I started to learn to dance at an early age, that training would help my feet turn out, and this would build even more strength in my muscles, along with teaching my entire body how to move correctly and gracefully.

She knew that all this had to be done. That it was going to be a few years of discomfort, and of whining and complaining, but that this would be a tradeoff for a lifetime of being able to wear whatever shoes I wanted. So she stuck to her guns.

And ultimately, once again, she was right. All that physical manipulation that she did on my legs eventually paid off. By the time I was a teenager, I didn't have any issues with my legs or knees anymore.

After all those years of wearing a boring uniform and those ugly corrective shoes, I was eventually free to choose anything that I wanted, and I would come to appreciate that, too.

CHAPTER 13

Life Lessons

Everyone is a teacher, if only for a moment.

My mother didn't fit in anywhere as a little girl because she wasn't the right color. So she spent a lot of time by herself in the woods, where she would observe the animals and how they interacted. She saw that all creatures have a job. The ants have a job. The snails have a job. So do the flies and bees. She watched them and learned their habits and grew to understand the interconnectedness of Nature. And these are the things that she would talk to me about when I was a little girl myself.

"You know about the bees?" she would ask. (I'm not talking about the birds and the bees. The bees only!) You didn't want to get her started on the bees. Believe me! Never mind specials done by *National Geographic* about how invaluable bees are to the world. My mother already knew how important they were, as well as about pollination and how it helps balance Nature in so many ways. She also understood that there were natural predators for some animals, and how these predators served a purpose, too. Nature had a way of balancing itself. It didn't need humans to interfere.

I think that she learned about acceptance from watching how Nature functioned. How the ants would be over here, and the bees would be over there, and they all sort of went their own routes and did their own jobs, which were all equally important, even if they had completely different functions and purposes.

And when she saw humans not being able to do the same thing . . . well, she just didn't understand it. It didn't make any sense to her. Why would a human being want somebody else to not exist just because they looked different, acted differently, thought differently, believed in different things, or simply wanted other things in life? Insects don't do that. When you compared the real essence of Nature to human behavior, it didn't add up to her. "That just doesn't compute," she would say. "I just don't *get* it!"

When you're not accepted as a child because you were born a certain way, how can you possibly "get" that? How does a child understand that someone won't accept them just because their skin is a different color? It really *doesn't* compute.

I think her entire view of life was built on these foundations she formed as a little girl—what she thought was the right way to behave and what made sense to her. Unfortunately, most societies and people don't function the way she thought they should.

My mother's beliefs, of course, were beyond skin-deep and applied to more than just race. They could be extended to everyone who had ever felt they didn't "belong" and were treated as outcasts. Like the LGBTQ community. She could not understand why anyone discriminated against other people due to their sexual orientation.

"I do think that same-gender partners should be able to be married," she said, long before same-sex marriage became legal in many states. "Why not? If you share a life together, then who in the world should have anything to say about it?"

These were just a few of the views about tolerance that my mother expressed. And I think that they stemmed largely from her having studied Nature.

Looking back now on all of these things that my mother taught me, I see that many of them were learned while we were in our vegetable garden. One of the main reasons having land in Beverly Hills was so important to her was that it allowed her to be close to the soil and the earth. After all, her name was Eartha. She was happiest when her hands were in the dirt and she was one with Nature. The dirt itself served as a teaching ground for her.

We would spend hours in our garden together, and she would impart her wisdom. Not in a deliberate way, though. She didn't lecture. She didn't preach. It was always much more subtle than that. She taught just by being conversational.

For example, in the garden, I would often point out bugs, as children tend to do. There were always bugs crawling around. Bugs, and snails, and slugs. The slugs, in particular, were fascinating to me. Fascinating in a slimy, creepy kind of way, I mean. An attractive species, they are not. Who likes slugs? So when I saw one, I would always say, "Kill it, Mommy! Eeewwww!"

And my mother would shake her head. "You don't 'Eeewwww!' anything," she would tell me. "Nothing is 'Eeewwww!'"

"You don't have to like it," she would go on to explain. "But you certainly don't have the right to kill it either, just because you don't like the way it looks."

Think about the power of that statement.

The same thing went for spiders. Spiders, to her, were God's insect killers. She thought they were among the greatest things on earth. As for spiderwebs? Well, that's how you got rid of flies. Nature's insect repellent. Beautiful, intricate structures that demonstrated the magnificent artistry of the natural world. She felt the same way about hornets' nests and beehives. My mother believed that everything in Nature served a purpose. So, just because we humans didn't want to have spiderwebs in our house didn't mean that they didn't have a right to be there.

Now, don't get me wrong. There weren't spiderwebs all over our house. All I'm saying is that my mother taught me tolerance at the most basic level. She taught me that just because you don't like the way something looks—or the way that it smells, what it eats, or how it behaves—doesn't mean that it isn't meant to be on this planet.

For a little child, this was an amazing lesson about acceptance. People always say things like, "We have to *lovvvve* each other!" Well, my mother wasn't about that. For her, it was that we *have to allow each other to exist.* That doesn't mean we have to love everything that everybody else does. Or embrace others' beliefs as our own. But we don't have the right to belittle other people or get rid of them just because they look or behave or believe differently from the way we do. She taught me to respect everyone. And not just everyone. *Every living thing.*

CHAPTER 14

Flower Child

It's not the number of books you've read,
it's the common sense you've gained.

As much respect as I may have learned to have for others, my mother also taught me that what is most important in life is not who, but *what* you know.

Yes, working in the entertainment industry, my mother knew a lot of famous people. But they didn't necessarily come over to our house. In many ways, she was a little reclusive. When she wasn't working—whether it be a play, film, recording session, or concert—she liked her privacy. And she liked to be home with me.

When I was young, we often watched old movies together. "I was born twenty years too late," I always said to her. "I should have been born in the 1930s or '40s." Bette Davis, Katharine Hepburn, Humphrey Bogart, and Fred Astaire were among our favorites. Also, Shirley Temple movies, the ones in which she would do tap-dancing routines with Bill Robinson, one of the first successful black actors. And *Gone with the Wind*—we could recite lines of dialogue from that one. I grew up watching all those movies with my mother. And she would usually have some anecdotal entertainment industry story she would share as we watched.

We really loved old musicals, too. Her favorite may have been *Guys and Dolls.* She and Marlon Brando, who played Sky Masterson in it, were friends, and I went to school with his son, Miko. It has been said that he and my mother were once an item, but I don't believe there was ever any real romance between them. Not as far as I know.

Bringing Up Baby with Cary Grant and Katharine Hepburn—that was certainly one of my favorites. I was a huge Katharine Hepburn fan and I loved every movie she was in. I thought she was so beautiful. And Bette Davis, too, although my mother would say they weren't considered real beauties in their day. I not only thought they were beautiful, but also admired the strong, sometimes complex women that they portrayed onscreen.

My mother didn't know most of these actors personally. But I do have a very cool photo of her with Cary Grant and Cab Calloway on the studio lot, taken when she and Mr. Calloway were filming the movie *St. Louis Blues.* My mother came to Hollywood in the '50s, when the studio system was still in effect. She was a part of that realm because that's what celebrities did at the time.

But those "Hollywood" encounters were just a snippet of who my mother was, and had little to do with us or with what she considered the most important things in life.

The important life lessons were often learned in the most unexpected moments. One, in particular, came at a very young age.

As I mentioned, my mother often performed in the Persian Room at the Plaza Hotel in New York. Once, when I was only about three or four, somebody gave her this huge bouquet of flowers. That's what many people do. They send flowers to celebrities.

I was little more than a toddler, and I must have gone up to this big bouquet of flowers and thought that the petals looked cool. And what do little kids sometimes do with flowers? You pick a petal, and you look at it, and then you pick another and you look at that one. Little kids are curious.

Apparently, I was *very* curious. I picked a lot of petals from this bouquet, and soon there were petals scattered all over the floor. Then my mother walked in and she saw what I had done.

So, what did she do? She didn't scream. She didn't yell. She didn't ask, "What did you *do?*" She walked calmly over to me, sat on the floor, and started picking up the petals one at a time.

I don't remember exactly what kind of flowers these were, but I think they were chrysanthemums. They had skinny little petals.

My mother placed each petal gently in her hand, and tears started to stream down her face.

I watched her as she quietly picked up every last one.

Finally, she spoke. "Each one of these petals is a baby," she said. "These petals are all the little babies. And the center parts of the flowers? They are the mommies. You just separated all of the babies from their mommies."

Whoa! Had she missed something in Parenting 101? Talk about motherly guilt. Freud would have had a field day with this one.

But that was my mother's method of teaching. Making connections. Emotionally. That was her way of making me understand how things in Nature are all connected to each other, and that you don't destroy them just because that's what you want to do. And that everything has a purpose.

Was it a traumatic event? Yes.

Was it an overdramatization? Absolutely. My mother was an actress, after all, and she was nothing if not dramatic.

But I sure as hell never destroyed another flower again. Lesson learned. You can check that one off, Mom!

Yes, it was an extreme way to make her point, but that's how my mother was. She acted things out because on some level she understood that the way you connect with children is to teach them a lesson. You have to make sure you express yourself in a way that they will understand. And that was one thing that I definitely understood.

Being separated from my mother was something that I couldn't have handled. So, to think that I had just destroyed this entire family. . . . What could have been worse?

It probably took me twenty years of therapy to get over that one. Maybe I'm still getting over it.

But that was the way that my mother operated. To her, everything was a teaching moment. Every experience offered something valuable to be learned.

What I realized as I got older and became a mother myself was that, if that had been my child, I would have walked into the room, looked down, and screamed, "What are you *doing?*" And my kid would have frozen in his or her tracks and ended up in tears.

I would have howled, like any parent would, "You don't ever do that to a flower!"

But if you think about the emotional connection that my mother made with me through the use of drama, and telling me a story, it offered a much deeper lesson than it would have if she had come in and scolded me or punished me in any way.

From that moment on, I always treated plants, flowers, and every other living thing, for that matter, gently and with the utmost care. The lesson that my mother instilled in me was that the flowers I had destroyed had been alive. They had been living things. Not simply that she had come in and screamed at me because I'd been doing something that I wasn't supposed to do.

Just remember where she came from. She didn't have any role models. Her parenting style was to use her instincts and operate purely on a gut level.

I learned all of these lessons well.

CHAPTER 15

Miss Kitt Goes to Washington

*We cannot defend freedom abroad
if we don't have it at home.*

As a young person, about the last thing I wanted to hear was my mother being political. Especially when she was as outspoken as my mine was.

My mother was truly a trailblazer in many ways, but one reason she felt so strongly about taking a stand was that she didn't see her "actions" as blazing a trail. She saw them as doing her civic duty and exercising her human rights. She felt that the U.S. Constitution and the Bill of Rights gave her the freedom of speech, so if she was asked for an opinion, then she was entitled to express it.

And she chose to express one of her strongest opinions during the Vietnam War, right inside the White House.

Let's just say that this didn't go over too well.

At the height of the war, my mother was invited to attend a luncheon for "women do-ers" at the White House on January 19, 1968, held by the then-First Lady, Lady Bird Johnson. Its purpose was to discuss a major issue then facing the country: "Why is there so much juvenile delinquency in the streets of America?" The guest list consisted of fifty women, many of whom were leaders in neighborhood anti-crime initiatives. The White House had wanted to include a celebrity. Someone had suggested my mother.

While in Washington, D.C., touring with the play *The Owl and the Pussycat* a year or two earlier, my mother had been approached by a group called Rebels with a Cause. Its mission was to help get unemployed youngsters off the streets and channel their energy in a more positive direction. My mother considered this to be important and readily agreed to help. She enlisted the aid of Roman Pucinski, a Democratic congressman from Chicago she had once met. Later, when Congressman Pucinski was asked by Mrs. Johnson's staff if he knew of any Hollywood celebrities involved with fighting juvenile delinquency, he in turn recommended my mother.

Good choice! Growing up in the South, my mother had always felt that she had no voice herself. For that reason, she related deeply to the downtrodden—those who felt hopeless and believed they didn't have a future. She not only supported their cause, but related to it. Having grown up in poverty herself, my mother personally connected to the need to help young people and give a voice to all those who would otherwise not be heard. So, when she was invited to the White House, she was eager to attend.

Once she arrived at the ladies' luncheon, though, she was appalled to discover that most of her fellow guests were evidently not there to help effect change. Everyone around her was busy oohing and ahhing over the table settings, and squirreling away the printed menus into their purses to take home as souvenirs. They appeared to be more interested in seeing who else was in attendance and fawning over the First Lady.

My mother was even more incensed hearing what many of the other guests had to say when they took the floor. Most of the speakers spent their time at the microphone congratulating Mrs. Johnson for what my mother considered to be more superficial public works projects that she had spearheaded, such as the 1965 Highway Beautification Act, which limited billboards on major roadways.

Lady Bird gave a speech herself. "The success of freeing our neighborhoods from hoodlums and fear depends upon the cooperation of all our citizens," she said.

My mother couldn't believe her ears. "I hadn't flown several thousand miles to hear Mrs. Johnson tell us how privileged we were to be there or that we should support our local police or that crime prevention begins at home. . . ," she later wrote.

And so, when Mrs. Johnson finally gave my mother a turn to express her opinion, she did just that. "The children of America are not rebelling for no reason," she told the gathered crowd. They were protesting against the war and their being drafted to serve in it, for it was a war that most young people did not support. Yet their objections were not being addressed.

"You send the best of this country off to be shot and maimed," she declared. "They don't want to go to school because they're going to be snatched off from their mothers to be shot in Vietnam."

I can only imagine the gasps around the room. Or was there shocked silence?

The New York Times would later report that, upon hearing this, the First Lady's "voice trembled and tears welled in her eyes." The story claimed that my mother had raised her voice and spoken to Mrs. Johnson in anger. It went on to add many more colorful details.

"Miss Kitt, her eyes flashing in defiance while she puffed on a cigarette and jabbed a finger at her startled audience, said . . . that youngsters feel alienated because 'they can't get heard by you and they can't speak to the President,'" and so there were protests in the street.

By that night, the name "Eartha Kitt" was all over the news, both on television and in print. And not just the local news. It became a national story, soon to be international.

Although the Kent State shootings would not occur for two more years, anti-war protests by students and others were becoming widespread by then. Other celebrities had also begun to voice their opposition publicly, including Jane Fonda, Norman Mailer, Paul Newman, Muhammed Ali, Joan Baez, and Johnny Cash.

"But the most direct and powerful anti-war statement of the period was delivered by singer Eartha Kitt, then at the height of her celebrity," an article later published in *The Nation* would assert.

Lady Bird's profile on the website FirstLadies.org appears to agree. "Kitt's remarks shocked the public; no such previous type of incident had occurred in the White House, let alone been intended for a First Lady who had no direct responsibility for the policy being questioned," it says.

Years later, of course, I have come to appreciate what my mother did, and the courage it took to stand up for what she believed in. At the time, however, I didn't understand what a big deal this was, nor the impact of my mother being so outspoken. Being only six at the time, I probably didn't know what had occurred at all. But as I got older, I often felt uncomfortable with her need to always speak her mind.

"Why do you need to be so political?" I would ask her. "Please, just don't say anything!" I didn't want to be the kid with the mother everyone talked about.

Now people, including myself, look back on her actions as being courageous. There were many others who felt the same way she did back then; they just didn't state it as publicly. They admired my mother for standing up to "the Establishment," but didn't dare do it themselves. Years later, while accompanying my mother to an event in Philadelphia at a small Sunday afternoon brunch, I heard something that I'll never forget. An older gentleman (probably around 80), approached my mother and told her that as a young Black child, growing up in Philly, he was moved to tears when she stood up to make a statement at the White House. He said that it was the first time that he, or any other young African American, had heard of any Black person standing up for "his people." His eyes filled with tears as he recalled his pride in her taking such a courageous stand. I will never forget his words.

Yet there were others who viewed what she had said as being anti-American because she appeared to be going against the government. For that reason, she paid a big price for feeling compelled to "speak her truth." Many of her upcoming engagements after the incident were soon canceled without explanation. And before long, she found herself blacklisted and unable to find work in the U.S. for many years to come.

The thing is, my mother had a very special way of speaking. I'm not just talking about the unique, unmistakable sound of her voice. If my mother had an opinion about something, she was most likely passionate about it, and it often came out that way. She didn't have anything against the First Lady personally. In fact, she always contended that she hadn't actually made Lady Bird cry at the luncheon. If she had cried, my mother said, it hadn't happened in front of her.

My mother felt very strongly about our involvement as a nation in the Vietnam War, though, and she would have liked for the president himself to have been present at the luncheon so she could have spoken to him directly. Yet he had only made a brief appearance before the event, for a photo op with the guests.

They did meet that day, at that photo op, though. There's a famous photograph of the two of them facing each other. A powerfully symbolic image, it looks very much like David versus Goliath, if David had been a compact Black woman from South Carolina and Goliath a strapping cowboy in a suit. My mother was a tiny little thing, and President Johnson towered over her. I often think of this image and how she must have felt, standing toe to toe with the most powerful person in the world. And the nerve it must have taken to speak out against his policies.

Think about it. You've got the president of the United States, and there was my mother, challenging him. He was a very large man at six-foot-four, so size-wise he easily dominated her. Yet when you see her standing in front of him, you know that this was not a woman who was ever going to back down. When I see that photo, I think, "Whoa! She had the conviction to speak honestly, no matter what! My mother was not going to be intimidated by anybody!"

That was my mother, Eartha. She was outspoken without ever having to speak loudly. She was feisty, but in a quiet, "Don't mess with me!" sort of way. This was the kind of impact she had. She was small in stature, yet the way that she carried herself showed that she was a woman of power. And you felt it!

People would be amazed when she walked into a room to see how small she was. Audience members who had just seen her perform onstage would often say to her, "I thought you would be at least five-eight or five-nine." But she was barely five-foot-two. Her presence was larger than life.

CHAPTER 16

Travels with my Mother

The river is constantly turning and bending, and you never know where it's going to go and where you'll wind up.

Years later, when Watergate was unfolding, it came to light that President Johnson, not his wife, was the one who had actually taken the most offense at what my mother had said about Vietnam. He had issued an order to the C.I.A. the following day to investigate her. He also put the word out to TV stations and production companies that he didn't want to see "that woman" anywhere. Reporter Seymour Hersh of *The New York Times* would call my mother several years later, in 1975, to reveal that after the C.I.A. had failed to uncover any notable scandals or evidence of un-American activities, the president had ordered the agency "to come back with something on that woman, I don't care what it is," as she would say.

The story in the *Times* would quote her as calling the investigation "disgusting" and having said, "I've always lived a very clean life and I have nothing to be afraid of and I have nothing to hide."

Unaware at the time of what was transpiring behind the scenes, though, my mother merely noticed that her engagements for work in the U.S. were drying up. Or, as she would later recount to Charles Osgood during that 2005 segment of CBS *Sunday Morning,* "Within two hours, I was out of work in America."

My mother had suspected that there was some sort of governmental interference in her career, but learning the truth simultaneously exasperated her and fueled her determination to persevere. It certainly didn't change who she was. Her attitude was, "You just keep moving forward, no matter what." Besides, this setback wasn't that different from other obstacles she had faced in her life. Fortunately, she wasn't famous just over here. Having long ago made a name for herself in Europe, and then continuing to tour worldwide, she also had an immense international following. So, as work dried up in the U.S., the door opened for her to appear at venues overseas.

Remember, my mother not only knew how to sing in seven languages; she also spoke four of them. So we continued to travel the world. Germany, Australia, South America, South Africa. . . . You name it, we probably were there.

My mother didn't just love to travel. She understood that when you have an opportunity to see other cultures firsthand, you should learn about them as much as you can while you're there. For that reason, she felt that it was very important to be multilingual. This was not only about being able to converse with people in foreign countries. Learning new languages also stimulated your brain, she believed. But mostly, it was a way for her to really get to know and understand the customs, beliefs, and traditions of other cultures and people, which in turn gave her the ability to make true connections with them.

For this reason, in every country that she visited she always made it a point to learn at least one of their songs. She not only sang in impeccable French, but also in Hebrew, German, Japanese, and Turkish. The songs that she learned, though, were not necessarily current songs that one would hear on the radio. More often, they were popular folk songs that everyone knew and loved. While in the Philippines, for example, she learned a song in Tagalog, one of its main regional languages. I know someone who grew up in the Philippines, and his elderly mother-in-law remembers her own mother singing that song to her when she was a little girl.

These were the kinds of songs that my mother looked for. Ones that were important or had historic relevance. Songs that touched people on a deeper level. Doing this was also a way for her to fit in immediately wherever she went. And not just to fit in, but to be welcomed and embraced.

You stand up on a stage in a foreign country as an American—especially an American person of color—and all of a sudden you throw in a song that's unique to their land, ethnicity, or culture? Do that, and people are instantly drawn to you. Take "Uska Dara," the song that my mother made famous and performed in Turkish throughout her career. She had learned it when she first performed in Turkey, and the audiences couldn't believe that she sang it in Turkish! Knowing the local lingo changes how people respond to you. No question.

Similarly, when my mother went to Israel, she not only learned some Hebrew, but Yiddish as well. Yiddish is a language that was spoken by many European Jews, so people have a deep connection to it. They say, "Oh, my grandmother spoke Yiddish." That grabs them on an emotional level. A very deep emotional level—one of the many reasons my mother's fans were (and still are) so devoted to her.

She instinctively understood the value of making true connections with others. But this wasn't done to impress people. My mother yearned for the energy that those deeper connections fostered.

And she was like a sponge. She wanted to absorb everything around her and to learn how other people lived. She was passionate in her belief that if human beings would make the effort to learn and understand each other, then our interactions would be so much more pleasant and peaceful. So, wherever we went, she would seek out people, from the hotel staff to taxi drivers and restaurant workers, and ask them questions. "Where are you from? Where do you live? Where do you shop?" She had never finished high school, but her insatiable thirst for knowledge made up for that. As a voracious reader, she wanted to know everything about the places we went and the people who inhabited them.

Yes, museums are really important, and we visited many of them, of course. So are churches and other houses of worship, because they tell so much about the history of a country and its society. But my mother didn't go into churches searching for religion. She wanted to know about the local history. Who were the people who had built them? What did they believe? What did they practice? What did they do, and why? These were the kinds of teachings she sought out, and to which I, in turn, was exposed.

Even more essential to her was learning about how the people in a place lived and functioned day to day. She did this by going into people's homes, and visiting their local markets. Inquiring about their customs and the different foods they ate, and why they ate them. She wanted to understand what their traditions and rituals were. She had a tremendous desire to truly learn about the world in which we live.

When she visited Australia, for example, she wanted to see how the Aboriginals lived and listen to their concerns. She wanted to hear about their history and the travails they had gone through. And she did that almost everywhere she visited—asked questions to which she really wanted to know the answers. I guess when your name is Eartha, you want to learn about the entire planet Earth, not just the little part of it where you were born.

I think there are certain people who are naturally curious, on a very grand scale. My mother was one of those people. Her curiosity was insatiable. And she imparted that to me. OK, maybe I don't have an inquisitive nature quite to "Eartha level," but in many ways

I didn't need to have that much curiosity, because she had enough for both of us.

My mother, as I said, wanted to learn about social and political issues, both foreign and domestic, so when she would converse with people in different countries, she would often ask their opinions of their governments. In that way, she grew to be very opinionated about what works and what doesn't.

I think that she had a right to her strong opinions because she did a lot of research to find out what other people thought, and she came to her own perspective by putting many different points of view together. It was like she created a big soup, a giant goulash of opinions, and she would stir it around and come to her own conclusions.

It was largely for this reason that she didn't enjoy talking about trivial matters. She only wanted to have real, deep conversations. She yearned for honest exchange.

In most places we went, we stayed in hotels, but we also had a house in London, because my mother was often there performing. Having a home base abroad made it easier to travel as frequently as she did through Europe, as well as the Far East and Africa. She toured so many different countries that I don't remember them all.

But I do remember that no matter where we went, the moment that we landed, my mother would insist on taking me out to explore.

I look back now and realize how incredible those experiences were. We had amazing adventures together and truly saw the world. But I wasn't always a willing participant. Obviously, as a little girl, I had no choice but to accompany my mother wherever she went, but as I got older. . . . Well, let's just say that I, too, had some strong opinions.

In many ways, I was a fairly typical little girl, and then became a typical teenager. I wanted to be in the hotel watching television with the air-conditioning on. The last thing I was interested in was being dragged to a museum. Or a church. Or to see the district of such-and-such.

So it was not as if all these incredible travels were Nirvana, and I was taking it all in and thinking, "Oh, how wonderful this is!" No, my mother often literally dragged me to all of these places. I wasn't given an option. It was, "This is what we're doing," and that's all there was to it.

Typical was when we went to Hong Kong in 1974. My mother was performing at the luxurious Mandarin Oriental Hotel, something that she had done many times before. But this time, it being summer and school vacation, I was allowed to bring a friend.

Flying into Hong Kong, there was an issue with the weather, though, so we were diverted to Bangkok, where the airline put us up in some hotel. The next day, there was a big backup of planes at the airport from the delays of the day before. We weren't going to be able to take off until sometime late in the afternoon. So my mother, never one to be sedentary, woke us up at some ungodly hour, like 6 A.M., and announced, "We're in Bangkok. We're going to take advantage of being in a new city. We're going to see the sights!"

The sights? It was 104°F outside and about 9,000 percent humidity. I didn't want to see any sights! This was crazy talk! But off we went. My protestations left to be heard by no one.

My mother immediately started a conversation with the taxi driver and asked where he shopped for food. (Big surprise!) He took us to an open-air market a few minutes away, which was unlike anything I had ever seen before. Animal carcasses were hanging everywhere, and live fish were still flapping around in many of the vendor stalls lined up side by side along a path. There were live chickens being slaughtered over here, and all sorts of strange vegetables and fruits over there. The air was thick with unfamiliar aromas. As for the heat? Well, it was overwhelming. Flies and other bugs were swarming throughout. And my mother was in her glory. Soaking up all of the sights and sounds, eager to participate in the hustle and bustle surrounding us.

I guess the cabdriver spoke English, so she took him through the market with us. He translated as she went around, asking everyone about all of the food, and where this came from and that came from. But I was only twelve at the time, and all I wanted was to be back in the hotel, watching TV in the comfort of our air-conditioned room while waiting for the plane to take off.

As I look back on it now, I think, "What an amazing experience—to have seen Thailand first-hand and observed what real life was like in such a foreign country." But at that moment I was just a miserable teenage girl. And anyone who has raised teenage girls knows exactly how miserable they can be.

How did my mother deal with that—teenage girl behavior? Well, there was nothing to deal with. There was no whining. Whining was not an option. You just sat there, quietly miserable in your own skin. I probably could have gotten away with complaining once or twice, saying, "I really don't want to do this." But I'm not sure that she would have acknowledged my plea. At best, she probably would have said something like, "I know. I'm sorry. But this is what we're doing." More likely, it wouldn't even have been addressed at all.

The option wasn't open for me to do something different. So why waste my breath? She wouldn't have gotten angry. She wasn't someone who often got mad. All she would have done was turn around and look at me. She would have given me *that look*. That's all that it ever took. One look.

Here's the thing about my mother: She parented on instinct. And her instinct told her that she had the opportunity to expose her child to situations where I would learn things I could never learn in a classroom. So I might as well keep quiet and go along for the ride.

The truth was that she had a way of making me want to comply with her agendas and rules. She would often hold my hand when we were walking, and there were times when I would say something and she would squeeze it, or turn around and look at me. And that was enough to stop whatever words were about to come out of my mouth.

That was also just a function of the era in which we lived. Children were expected to do as they were told when I was growing up. With my own kids, I worry about what they think. But when my mother's generation was in charge, children didn't get to negotiate. Nope. It was, "This is what we're doing. This is what you're eating for dinner. This is not a restaurant; we're not having six different choices. This is what we're eating, this is what we're doing, and that's just how it is."

It was a different time. Adults didn't give kids choices. The current generation is given options, including the option to just say no and opt out.

It didn't matter that my mother was famous. I wasn't ever given the option to opt out. Her attitude was that you don't get to opt out in life when things don't go your way. And if you do, you're missing the point. Life, after all, is not about everything being perfect. It's about being able to be happy in the moment, or at the very least content. It's about finding whatever happiness you can.

One needs to be willing to go with the flow. Which is the opposite of opting out.

"You have to be willing to adapt," she would say, "or life is going to be miserable." I remember my mother telling me that time and time again. "You've got to learn to adapt, kid. You've got no choice." That was not easy to hear. Especially for an only child used to being fawned over by her mother. I didn't want to hear, "Suck it up. This is what you are doing." I wanted to hear, "You can take a nap, or do whatever else you want." But she didn't let me get away with that kind of stuff. To her, there were lessons to be learned, experiences to have, and LIFE TO LIVE!

There is also another very important part of life, I learned, which is death.

Death, aside from the sadness and permanent loss, is in some ways really fascinating. The rituals that different people, religions, and societies have surrounding death are so important. I now understand more than ever just how important they are.

My mother showed that to me at different times in my life when something had happened and death was around us—whether it be that a goldfish had died, or a furry pet, or a family member or friend.

During that memorable trip in 1974, when my mother was performing in Hong Kong, a situation occurred across the street from our hotel, where they were building a giant skyscraper. One day, I was standing out on the balcony, which overlooked the harbor. A group of men were working out on the scaffolding, when suddenly it broke. Two of the men managed to grab hold of something, but two others fell.

Fell to their death, right in front of me.

I was only twelve, and needless to say, it was a horrifying experience. But to my mother, again, everything in life was an opportunity to learn something. In the ensuing days, all sorts of religious rites and rituals surrounding this tragic moment could be observed unfolding at the base of that building. People continued to come and go, and there were fires being burned, and little pieces of paper they would burn in those fires.

My mother began to ask members of the hotel's housekeeping staff about it. "What's happening? What are they doing? Why are they doing that right where the bodies landed?" It wasn't about making me experience something that was horrible. It was about teaching me, and educating herself, about how other people do things and what they believe.

She had me listen to what was being explained about all the rituals following these deaths. My mother wanted me to know and understand what the Chinese believed. We learned that the pieces of paper that were put into those fires were in the shape of money. The belief was that this was a means for the deceased men's families to safeguard their departed spirits by paying their way into Heaven.

Here was this horrifying experience for a young person, or anyone, really, to see, but my mother turned it into a learning opportunity. Curiosity was something she possessed in infinite abundance and wanted to cultivate in me. You know how they always talk about curiosity and the cat? Well, my mother was nothing if not feline. She was endlessly curious about why people did things and always wanted to know more.

Only much later would I fully appreciate what an advantage for me that would be. How you learn to adapt and approach the path in front of you is what determines your level of happiness. I think this is one of the most vital lessons I learned from my mother.

There are many situations in my life where I can roll with the punches, and so they don't faze me at all. That's an invaluable quality, I think, even if it's not easy to instill as a parent.

My daughter Rachel was once doing a service project in Australia while she was in high school, and soon after she arrived, she called to say that she had broken a toe.

"Well," I replied, "you've got nine other toes, and you're all the way in Australia. Don't waste the trip, and please drink more water." (That last part is a private joke in the family. Whenever anything bad happens, I always say, "You need to drink more water.")

"Ma," she replied in frustration, "I broke my toe! I don't need to drink more water."

"Is it going to *hurt* you to drink more water?" I asked. "Drink more water!"

There are times in life when you need to make the best of a difficult situation. You have no choice. That's another important lesson that my mother taught me.

She also taught me to drink more water.

As for Rachel, I must admit that she also complained when she arrived in Israel on a Birthright trip. She said that there were bugs in the hotel, and the shower was dirty.

Bugs in the hotel? Dirty shower? Just wear your beach shoes in the bathroom, I told her. That's life! Try to enjoy yourself. You'll just have a good story to tell someday.

OK, maybe that was my mother speaking through me, to some extent. She would have been the first to say, "You've got nine other toes. Relax, move on, and try to enjoy yourself!"

Actually, I don't know if I would have dared to call my mother to tell her that I had broken a toe. Thanks to her, I was more independent than most young teenagers. *Much* more independent. As young as thirteen, I could easily take care of myself. I could have taken care of a whole battalion if I needed to. I was very good at taking the lead.

That, to a large extent, is because knowing my mother's story, and seeing her pain whenever she would retell it, I often felt like I was the parent. In the feline world, Mother Lions are fiercely protective of their cubs; in our own little cat world of two, this cub was extremely protective of her mother.

CHAPTER 17

A Fox in the Kitt House

For the mind to wander is not necessarily a bad thing.

I was counting the painted floor tiles, purposefully placing each foot heel to toe, creating a soothing rhythm as I walked. I loved the way that my newly straightened feet filled the party shoes, every toe snuggled into a space of its own. Since being freed from my corrective shoes, I looked for every opportunity to wear my patent-leather Mary Janes. And that morning in Vienna, when my mother announced that we were going to visit yet another church, I knew that dressing nicely would meet with her approval. For a woman who didn't believe in organized religion, she sure made me visit a lot of churches when we traveled.

My mother always seemed to enjoy learning about a town or city's history through its places of worship when we were abroad, but I have to say that I just found these excursions to be boring and repetitive.

Vienna Church No. 3 turned out to be no exception. It was cold and uninviting, its colors muted and drab. The floor tiles appeared to be almost tear-stained, as if the angels on the ceiling had been crying for hundreds of years. Soon enough, I felt ready to cry along with them.

I wandered down the center aisle, never too far behind the adults, their hushed voices softly bouncing off the stone walls and stained-glass windows. But all I could hear was the click-clack-click of my own deliberate "party shoe" steps.

The Vienna weather was damp and dreary, hanging over the city like a cloud of sadness, adding to the atmosphere of doom and gloom. My steps began to feel like a funeral march as I weaved my way through the heavy wooden pews. I felt like a dwarf in the cavernous structure, the intricately painted ceiling seeming as far away as the sky.

We were on a private tour, and except for one or two priests, I don't think there were any other people present. I followed behind, listening with only one ear to the information my mother was absorbing, preferring to come up with my own stories about the tombs and tapestries, sculptures and frescoes.

The walls were dull and the stained glass almost colorless, enhancing my disinterest. "Get. Me. Out. Of. Here!" were the words that echoed in my head with each click of my heels.

Near the altar, I came upon a pew with elaborate kneeling cushions designed for the ancient Austrian nobility, I imagined. Finally, the opportunity to take a much-overdue rest! Placing my knees on the padded platform, I was relieved to have found a passably comfortable spot. I folded my hands in prayer and pleaded with God to get my mother to speed up this tedious tour.

Then, as I pretended to be devout, I looked down and saw something on the ground right beside me. It was a tiny stuffed animal. But not your typical teddy bear or floppy-eared dog. This one was a fox, his ears frayed and his tail torn so that all of its stuffing was gone.

He, too, appeared to be praying. Praying to be rescued. Or maybe found.

"Hey, little guy, are you lost?" I asked. "Or were you left behind?"

I wrapped a gloved hand around his coarse, dirty blonde hair, his one remaining brown plastic eye dull with sorrow, as if he had been forgotten.

"I don't blame you for looking so sad," I said, stroking his well-worn face. "This isn't a place in which I'd want to be lost."

I sat back in the pew, no longer concerned with its rock hardness, my little companion distracting me from my boredom and surroundings. Not only was I pleased to have just rescued this mouse-like creature from a medieval dungeon, but I had found myself an instant friend.

Hearing my mother's voice coming closer, I clutched the little orphan to my chest and turned in her direction. "Look, mommy! Look!"

I held him high for all to see, his only eye in clear view. "He was lost! I found him on the ground, praying," I called to her elatedly.

My mother reached out, lifted his scruffy face, and stroked his furry head. I pointed out where I had made my discovery.

Never mind that I was breaking the unspoken rule of using only quiet church voices inside a house of worship. My mother smiled with wisdom at our newest family member. "A lost soul in a church, in search of salvation," she stated softly. "I think he came in here in search of a family. How lucky are you, Mr. Fox?"

My mother had always liked taking in strays, be they two-legged creatures or four. A stuffed rescue pet would be no exception.

Taking me by the hand, she placed my new traveling companion back in my care, knowing that I would now be more willing to stay by her side as we made our way to the next wing of Vienna's largest church.

My Austrian souvenir later flew home with us, and that is where he stayed. He sits on a shelf in my room, never to be forgotten and still adored to this day, looking just as well loved as on the day that I found him . . . or should I say we found each other?

CHAPTER 18

Growing Pains

When life becomes confused, step aside and think.

How do you learn about sex from a sex kitten? I would like to say I have a good answer to that question. But I'm not quite sure that I ever did. Learn about sex from her, that is. She spent much more time warning me, not so much about sex, but, rather, love. Preparing me for all the perils that it posed. "Don't ever be dependent on a man for anything," she would say to me again and again. "Never be dependent on other people." That may have been her No. 1 mantra.

Not that she needed to rein me in that much. I was a good girl. Even as a teenager. As I got older, I remained a good girl.

And a pretty conservative girl. I didn't run with a fast crowd. I didn't drink. Didn't do drugs. I never even stayed out past my curfew. Almost never, anyway. But there was one memorable time that I did.

As I said, I was one of those annoying children who was considered "the good kid." I was not an experimenter. I was not a risk-taker. I don't think my mother would have known how to deal with that. But she never had to. I will be the first to admit that I was a giant weenie and a coward.

But as I got older, I wasn't perfect. One night I slept over at a girlfriend's house, and we went to a party and stayed out well past our 11 P.M. curfew. As a result, my friend ended up getting grounded. Not me, though. I thought fast on my feet. And used the freedom of my own imagination . . .

When my mother asked me what had happened, I brainstormed and quickly came up with an explanation. I told her that we had stayed out so late because we'd had no way of getting home. We had gone to the party with some older boys, and they hadn't been ready to leave when we wanted to go. There were no Ubers at that time, of course. No such thing as Lyft. There were no buses, either. Taxis were even hard to come by. This was Southern California. We had no way of getting home.

Hearing this, my mother didn't get angry at me. She got angry at the situation. "You're never going to be put in that position again," she declared, "where you're dependent on somebody else to get someplace." Then she went out and bought me a car. Not a brand-new car. A used MG. It wasn't anything fancy.

I was only fifteen and a half at the time. You weren't allowed to drive in California until you were sixteen. But she bought me a car, anyway. She knew that I wasn't going to get caught breaking the law because I was a good driver. My ability to be independent was more important to her than my following a law.

When I think about that incident now, I can't quite believe she did that. When my own kids were old enough to get their learner's permits, then their licenses, I could barely stand to let them drive on the driveway. Whenever one of them would drive home from school, I would be waiting breathlessly until the door opened. But my mother wasn't like that.

Then again, I was one of those kids who was never going to get in trouble in any way. As I said, I didn't drink, and I didn't do drugs. So you weren't going to find me drinking and driving. The worst thing I ever did as a teenager was break that curfew.

I was also never going to be the kid who had a party and drove other kids around. First of all, I didn't have that many friends, and the ones I did have were almost as "boring" as I was. Since my friends and I went to a school where many of the students were from foreign countries, I think we were just much more conservative than most other kids. I also wasn't going to race, or do any other stupid things in the car. I mean, my mother knew that I was one of those kids whose head was set squarely on her shoulders.

I'm not saying that this justified her letting me drive at age fifteen and being a scofflaw. But she was more outraged that we were out with a group of boys who had driven us to a party and then wouldn't take us home. That, at least, was my story. That was not what my friend told her parents. As I said, I was pretty savvy. I was able to work the system. To this day, my friend still says, "I can't believe that I got grounded and you got a car!"

There were also other areas in which I was encouraged to exercise my independence. As I got older, I began to express more of my creativity and would dress in very unique ways.

When I wasn't wearing my school uniform, I enjoyed putting together outfits. This started, in fact, when I was quite little. My mother would pick out clothes for me, and I would say, "I don't want to wear that."

I remember that she put out an outfit for me once, and I just refused to put it on. She was not happy because she had gone to great lengths to go to some fancy store and purchase these clothes for me. We were going somewhere and it was important that I look nice. I was only about eight or nine. She became so upset that I finally said, "Fine!" Then I stormed off and put the outfit on, and when I came back in, she saw that I was, in fact, right. It *was* hideous. She broke into hysterical laughter. For years after that, she would recount the story of how, even at a very young age, I had known that outfit was dreadful and had refused to be seen in it.

But from that day forward, she decided that I knew what looked good on me and I could be trusted to know what to wear . . . and what *not* to wear.

After that, I would put unexpected pieces together and mix interesting colors, or put on a pin or throw a scarf around my neck, and my mother would always say to people, "Kitt has such an incredible sense of fashion! She really has her own style." I would beam with pride because, since I carried my mother's name, it was one of the ways I could demonstrate my individuality. And my mother encouraged that. My self-expression. My individuality. Even when I was an adult, she would often say to me, "You find the coolest-looking things to wear that work so well for you."

Then again, if I offered to buy one of those "cool" things for her, she would say, "No, that's OK." She, too, knew what fashion pieces suited her.

When I had kids of my own, I quickly learned that empowering your children with the freedom to make their own choices is not always easy to do. Sometimes my daughter would put together the craziest outfits. I remember my husband once saying about one of them, "You can't let her go out like that!" And I remember thinking, "It's not my style. But my style wasn't my mother's style, either." I now realize how difficult it must have been for my mother to hold her tongue about some of my wardrobe decisions. But, as I have noted, she understood the value of being able to keep her mouth shut.

CHAPTER 19

Ms. Manners

I have not rules, but guidelines.

My mother always stuck to her guns, as I have mentioned, and she was very strict. People are always surprised when I say that, because they tend to think of celebrities as being very liberal, allowing their children to do whatever they want. But my mother wasn't like that. She was quite strict, which could be intimidating, especially to young people.

It's not that my friends, who knew her, were actually scared of her. But she was a commanding presence, despite her diminutive stature, and she expected proper manners and respect from everyone, grownups and children alike.

She didn't like any form of profanity and would never use it herself. To curse was not ladylike. She wouldn't dare to say the word "sh-t," for example. If she was so upset about something that she needed to swear, she would say it in French. I guess she found that somehow less offensive.

"Please" and "thank you," on the other hand, were words that she longed to hear used more often. She felt that kindness was a lost art, and that good manners were simply a form of human decency.

But above all, as I have said, she was a stickler for good grammar. Funny for someone who had very little formal education. But as I have mentioned, my mother was an avid reader. And not of fiction. My mother understood the importance of language and words, and what is an effective way to learn about them? Reading the dictionary. Yes, you read that correctly. The Merriam-Webster, Oxford, or any other at hand. Her life circumstances had not allowed her the luxury of earning a degree, so self-growth became her life's work.

Sometimes I would say, "Can I have (such-and-such)?" And she would reply, "You can, but you need to ask if you *may*." Yes, I found that frustrating at times. I would wait till I was out of sight, and then roll my eyes, as any typical daughter would do.

My mother trusted me. And she encouraged my independence, creativity, and imagination. But that isn't to say she never criticized my behavior. I grew up in the 1970s, and sometimes as a teenager, when she asked me a question, I would say, "I dunno." And she would say, "I dunno? There's no such word as 'dunno.' It's 'I don't know!' 'Uh-huh' is also not a word! It's 'yes' or 'no!'"

She wasn't only demanding when it came to speech, though. She also expected me to observe proper etiquette—how you hold a fork and knife at the dining table, or address a person you are meeting for the first time, or behave in other social situations. Manners were very important, so she made sure that I learned them. That's why I went to cotillion, which was common back then. Certainly, more common than it is now. I was very young at the time, only about seven or eight, as I recall. This was back in the late '60s. The girls wore little white gloves, white patent leather shoes, and little white anklet socks. Quite the look.

I attended cotillion, as etiquette classes for children were known, with Nat King Cole's twin daughters, Timolin and Casey, who were almost exactly my age, and their brother, Nat Kelly Cole. I believe Vincent Price's daughter, Victoria, attended with us, too.

Although I attended cotillion, I didn't have a coming-out party, or anything like that, thank goodness. It wasn't the debutante aspect of the classes that was important to my mother. She felt that etiquette shows respect for yourself and the people around you by your being polite and thoughtful. Then again, that was a different era. Most people don't send their children to formal "charm school" classes anymore. But maybe they should. It sure does feel like we could all use a healthy dose of common decency.

I know the pride I feel as a parent when one of my kids shows that they are considerate or polite. I still remember one particular instance of this, when my son was only about thirteen or fourteen. I was dropping him at school, and when he got out of the car there was a girl walking into the building at the same time, and he held the door open for her. I called my husband right away from the car, and said, "Jason just held the door open for a girl! Can you believe it? He was listening! He *did* pay attention!"

My mother gave me the gift of knowing how to behave in almost any situation. She gave me social skills. This may sound trivial, but often it's the small things that can have the most impact. I was thinking recently, for example, about how unfortunate it is that there is less and less cursive handwriting used in our society. Cursive is becoming a thing of the past. Many school districts don't even teach it at all.

They also certainly don't teach kids how to write thank-you notes—an art form too often replaced nowadays with an email or text message (which are certainly better than nothing, but just don't pack quite the same memorable punch).

When our kids were younger, my husband had a young man who worked with him. He was probably twenty-three and was from the Washington, D.C., area. We invited him over for Thanksgiving dinner one year, because he didn't have anywhere to go. The next week, we received a handwritten thank-you note from him. It was a simple note, but very beautiful. And the first thing I said when it arrived was, "Oh, my gosh, his parents really taught him well!" That note hung on our bulletin board for at least ten years, until we redid the kitchen. And every single time one of my kids receives something that I think requires a thank-you note, I say, "I just want you to remember that Eric Rosenthal's note meant so much to me that, a decade later, it was still hanging in our kitchen."

It's funny how important these little things are to us. But they *are* important. That's one of the things we talk about as parents. We talk to our kids constantly about treating everybody kindly, and just being nice and caring toward others. Those things mean a lot. And they especially did to my mother.

Having had teenagers myself now, I know that most teens fight with their parents sometimes, or at least they can be moody and argumentative. Rebelling is a completely normal rite of passage. I didn't have that luxury, though. Fighting with my mother was fraught with conflict for me. I was all she had, and I knew that. I was afraid she would feel that I was turning on her. My mother had been obliged to "grow up" too fast to ever experience what it was like to be a teen herself. And she didn't have any parental role models to turn to for guidance or advice when dealing with a teenager.

But the truth was that, as I got older, fourteen or fifteen perhaps, I didn't want to travel with her as much anymore. I really wanted to be home more, be able to hang out with my friends, and have more of a normal childhood. My mother took this personally. She felt that when I chose to stay home, it was a personal rejection of her. She would say to people, "Now she just wants to be with her friends!"

And I remember feeling very guilty. "Oh, what a horrible kid I am! I want to be with my friends!" I would think, knowing that I really wasn't.

She didn't understand kids' behavior. *All* teenagers want to be with their friends. They want to be with other kids. Duh! They don't want to be with their mothers.

But I gave her so much stability, especially when she was out on the road. My mother wanted me to be with *her*. She needed me and was dependent on that.

It can be a burden to be your mother's best friend and constant companion. Sometimes, I wished that she wasn't who she was. I would think, "Why can't you be a teacher? Why do you have to be an entertainer? Why do you have to travel so much? Why can't you just stay home like other parents do?"

That was the point at which I most wished that I'd had a sibling or another parent to whom I could say, "Would somebody please explain to her that this is just normal? That that's exactly what you're supposed to do as a teenager—hang out with your friends?" That was something that she just didn't get. The rejection she felt as a little girl was always right there, ready to pop back out and rear its ugly head again.

That's what happened when I went to my friend Clara-Lisa's birthday party one Mother's Day. I think it was the year I turned fourteen. I still spent the whole morning with my mother before going to the party, and the whole evening afterward. But it didn't matter. She interpreted it as a sign of disrespect, and I was deeply hurt by it.

Don't punish me because my best friend in the whole world was having a birthday party and I wanted to go to it. That wasn't fair!

As a little girl, though, when I would listen to her stories and hear her talk about her childhood, it was so painful to hear about the way that she'd been treated that I never wanted to be someone who added to that pain in any way. So, many times, I would be the one who would bite my tongue

CHAPTER 20

R-E-S-P-E-C-T

I stayed on my path and did not follow the herd.
I made a way for myself.

I never sensed that, because I was a girl, I could only do certain jobs. My mother was an incredibly strong-willed woman, and also a physically strong one. For her, having good manners, displaying proper etiquette, and acting "ladylike" didn't mean you had to conform to society's ideas of what women can or cannot do or be.

Being a lady also certainly didn't make a woman any less capable than a man. Just like my mother, there was a brief time when I also liked to do needlepoint back when I was a teenager, and my favorite piece, which was framed inside my room, said, "A woman's place is in the House and the Senate too."

When we would watch those old movies with Katharine Hepburn and Bette Davis, they were always playing strong women. They were never subservient to anyone else, or playing second-class citizens. They were independent and powerful. As was my mother. My ultimate role model.

My mother would make a point of observing the way that they behaved. To say that they were "ladylike" would not be quite accurate. That implies that they were walking around curtsying to everybody, and things like that. Rather, they were classy. She considered it important to maintain a certain level of classiness. Especially if you were a woman. It was about the way you sat. The way you walked. You didn't have to be all dressed up, but you were not allowed to look slutty. You didn't ever look "cheap." You dressed like you respected yourself. That's what it really came down to.

Self-respect.

And you definitely didn't chew gum in public.

This didn't just apply to women, however. She expected men to behave like gentlemen, too. To hold the door open for her and pull out her chair. Of course, that was largely part of the era. Her generation learned to do that. In the '50s and '60s, that's what you did. A man held the door for a lady, and he stood when she entered the room.

That was all part of the respect that women were entitled to be shown back then. It didn't make you any less than equal to a man in her mind just because he held a door open for you. Doing that was just gentlemanly. It was kind. And my mother didn't feel that being treated this way took anything away from her strength as a woman.

In her view, women were lucky that they could allow such nice-ties without it detracting from their power in any way. She felt it was a beneficial thing to be a woman. You got to be strong, but you also got to have someone pull your chair out for you, or open the door and help you step out of a car.

Respect to her was not restricted to these "old-fashioned'" forms of courtesy, though. Respect was also about being on time. It was about learning your job, getting your work done, meeting your dead-lines, and being willing to always go that extra mile. If you were in the entertainment business, as my mother was, that meant knowing your script or your songs. Or if you were a student, you were expected to complete all of your assignments. Those things were etched in stone, as far as my mother was concerned.

So even after she was already a famous person, she would always be early. And if she wasn't early, then she sure as hell wasn't late. She would arrive at the theater for rehearsals twenty or thirty minutes ahead of schedule. Often, people much younger than her would only show up on time, or maybe even be late. When that hap-pened, my mother felt slighted. She thought it was disrespectful— to the rules of etiquette, and to the director, as well as the actors or staff members who'd shown up at the proper time.

I wish I could say that I learned that lesson well and am always fabulously on time. Or even early. But I always seem to be juggling several things at once, literally and figuratively . . . and that results in my always running a little behind schedule. My husband would say that if I were an airline, I would have a terrible on-time perfor-mance record. For the most part, I show up . . . pretty much nearly on time. But it remains a trait that I'm still working on. My mother was never a fan of my tardiness. She was always punctual herself. She hated being late.

On some level, I think this was also about her own safety and peace of mind. She didn't want to risk getting called out for any reason. Certainly not as a young girl. She tried her hardest to keep the attention off herself. To be invisible. And quiet. It was safer for her that way. She was already deeply conscious of having been identified as being of mixed race and illegitimate, and the mistreatment that that provoked. So she wanted to be able to control any other issues that she had it within her power to avoid.

In her later years, she was almost always the oldest person in the cast, and she expected people to know their lines, show up on time, be prepared, and not complain. She found it very frustrating that young people would often say, "I don't feel well," or "I couldn't do it last night, I was out too late." There was always some type of an excuse.

My mother, by contrast, never had an excuse and almost never missed a performance. The only exception to this that I remember happened one year when there was a terrible blizzard while she was doing the Broadway show *Nine*. The driver picked her up at her home in Connecticut, and they tried their best, but they just couldn't get there because of the incredible amount of snow. She was so upset that night. She felt that she had failed everyone. She hated to disappoint anyone, especially her fans.

She also always retained the feeling that, "I can't give anybody a window of opportunity to criticize or reject me." She wouldn't let anyone think that she didn't live up to expectations, or whatever the requirements were.

A lot of that was her personality. She was determined to show respect to people in general, and especially to whoever her boss was, be it the director, the producers, or the studio. But most of all, my mother felt that you always respected your elders.

Always!

She felt this to the point that, even at fifty or sixty years of age, if she met someone who was sixty-five or seventy, she would refer to them as Mr. or Mrs. [fill in name] until they said, "Oh, please call me Mary," or whatever their first name was. She never called anyone by his or her first name until she was given explicit permission to do so.

I always thought that was so old-fashioned. It *was* old-fashioned. That's certainly not how it is today. But that's what my mother believed. She said that, as an elder, a person was due respect from anyone who was younger.

That was one of the reasons that my mother called our long-time housekeeper "Mrs. McCoy" for our entire lives. Even though Mrs. McCoy worked for my mother, because she was her elder, my mother always referred to her as "Mrs. McCoy."

My generation was brought up that way, too. We didn't call an adult by his or her first name. I always called my friends' parents "Mr. and Mrs." They never expected their children's friends to refer to them in any other way. I'm not sure I even knew what my friend Jackie's mother's first name was. To me, she was always Mrs. Nesbit.

I do remember having a friend once who called her mother by her first name, and I thought that was so cool. I wanted desperately to call my mother by her first name, too. So I did. ONCE. And let's just say that was the last time I ever did that!

She just shot me one of those powerful looks. Calling her "Eartha" even once was more than enough to provoke that fiery glare.

"You don't EVER call me by my first name!" she said. "Ever! I am your mother! And that's what you call me."

I didn't call her "Mother," of course. I called her Mommy. As I got older, maybe from my late teens on, I called her Mom. There were also times when I would call her "*Maman*," which is French for Mommy. But I sure never called her Eartha again.

She, in turn, would often call me "Kittseleh." (It was like Bubbeleh, a popular term of endearment in Yiddish.) In fact, there are some videos taken behind the scenes in which you can hear her saying "Kittseleh" with what sounds like a Yiddish accent.

Where, you might wonder, did she pick that up? I recently found a journal that my mother wrote when she was in Tel Aviv and Haifa many years ago. She did a lot of work for Israel and for Israel bonds. She also had a lot of friends who were either Holocaust survivors or the direct descendants of Holocaust victims or survivors. Plus, Beverly Hills back in those days was predominantly Jewish, or sure felt like it. Many of the people who lived there were Jews from Manhattan or Brooklyn who had come to the West Coast to work in the entertainment business.

My mother not only had many Jewish friends, but also identified with them as a people who had been ostracized. She'd had friends who had made it through World War II who would keep their arms covered with long sleeves. They were ashamed of the number tattoos that they had been given by the Nazis in concentration camps. For that reason, she was always upset when she saw people who had actually chosen to get themselves tattooed. She thought, "Why would you ever want to mark yourself in the same way that others once used markings to brand people as property, the way that slaves were branded and Jews were stamped?"

She would actually say that. "There are Jews who were tattooed because they were being stamped with a number. Why would you ever do that to your own body?" That just bewildered her.

Now, I didn't have any tattoos as a teenager. It's become very trendy in today's world. But as a teenager, and young adult, I never wanted to get one.

But when I would hear her talk like that, I would say, "That's so old-fashioned. That's ridiculous! You're not even Jewish! And you weren't in a concentration camp."

And she would say, "No, but I know what it's like to be excluded because of something that's out of your control, or because of the way that you were born. I know what *that* feels like."

The truth is that I happen to have tattoos myself now. But by the time I got my first one, I was thirty-five and I already had a child. And no, she did not approve. But at that point, she realized there was really nothing she could do about it. She certainly couldn't control what I did to my own body. And she respected a woman's right to choose—to choose what she did with her own body, as well as what she put on it.

Still, she would continue to roll her eyes whenever she noticed it and say, "I just don't understand why you would do that to yourself. I just don't *get* it."

Despite that, that tattoo was not the last one I would get. I now have seven.

I already told you about the one on my wrist that says "Don't Panic." The one on my outer left arm says "Here's to Life." It's the name of a song written by Artie Butler and Phyllis Jean Molinary, with which my mother closed her concerts for many, many years. The funny thing is that when the tattoo artist did it, he accidentally closed up the "t," so it's in the shape of a heart. He didn't do that intentionally. He was trying to make a handwritten "t" in script, and the top and bottom of the "t" met, forming a heart.

Then, on my right hand, I have her handwritten heart, which she often penned on her letters. Whether or not she would have ever liked this one or not, it reminds me that she is always with me, and that fills my heart and soul, too.

CHAPTER 21

Fit for Life

I think that the best exercise is natural exercise.

ndestructibly seductive at 79" is what *The New York Times* called my mother while she was performing at the Café Carlyle in 2006. Part of that seductiveness was her flirtatious, kittenish stage persona. But another big part was the incredible shape that she was still in. And she owed that to her exercise regimen and healthy eating habits. She did what it took to stay in shape. She worked out every day. It's hard for me to remember a single day when she didn't do some sort of physical activity.

As a performer, my mother needed to stay fit in order to maintain her stamina onstage and look her best. But to her, it was more fundamental than that. Staying fit and healthy—both physically and mentally—was absolutely essential. And she made those things a major priority throughout her life.

There's something to be said for genetics, of course. My mother was clearly blessed with good genes. But being a petite little thing, she still ate sparingly and exercised every day.

She wasn't one to necessarily need a gym, though. She believed that natural exercise was the best exercise by far. "What do you always need a gym for?" she would say. "Why do you need all of that equipment? Go jump over a log. Go run in the park. You have a world of nature out there!" (Again, she was "of the earth.")

She preferred working out in natural habitats. In Denmark, we often stayed with a family in a little town called Holte. While there, we would frequently go into the forest, where there was an obstacle course created entirely from nature. You would follow this numbered path, and when you came to each number on the path there would be a diagram of the exercise you were supposed to do on the apparatus that had been created. For example, if the exercise was to do chin-ups or pull-ups, there would be a tree cut and a piece of wood placed horizontally. Elsewhere on the course, you'd have to jump over a tree trunk. There was also a different station you could use for step-ups. It was a very cool spot.

Even at home, though, my mother turned to the natural world for exercise. Back when I was growing up, she would go to the Santa Monica beach and run. And not just in good weather. Every single day! In California, the weather is almost always good, so you could swim and be outside pretty much all year round. My mother didn't run on the hard, packed sand by the water, though. She preferred the soft, dry sand away from the water, which is much harder on your legs. And even that wasn't challenging enough for her. She would do this with a weighted backpack strapped to her back.

When I was little, she would drop me off at school in the morning and then drive straight to the beach. Or sometimes I would go to the beach with her before school, at 6 A.M., and I would sit in the empty lifeguard stand while she ran, eating my peanut butter and jelly on whole wheat toast (a favorite of mine to this day). That's what Mrs. McCoy made me for breakfast.

Mrs. McCoy, as I said, was our housekeeper. She had previously worked for the comedian Danny Kaye and his family. Then she worked for Diahann Carroll and her family. Then she worked for us. I think she was with us for seventeen or eighteen years.

I was not someone who was raised to think that other people were around to pick up after me, though. No, my mother wouldn't have allowed that. I had chores. I was expected to keep whatever area of the house I was in tidy. I had to clean my own room. And make my own bed. My mother's feeling was, "Mrs. McCoy is here to help me take care of the house. You are perfectly able-bodied. You can keep your own room clean."

Nor could I ever have given instructions of any kind to anyone who worked for us. Not once. Not for a split-hair of a second! If any adult I knew told me to do something, then, since I was a kid, I was expected to do it. And if I didn't like it, then I could talk to my mother about it, not to the person who had given me those instructions.

Not that I ever would have considered talking back to anyone. Especially to Mrs. McCoy. Oh, did I love Mrs. McCoy! And she loved me, too. And showered me with affection. I'm sure she felt somewhat like a mother to my mother. She was very protective of us both. A tall, sweet woman, she towered over my mother and always stood with her shoulders back and her chest out, as if she had served in the military (although I don't believe she ever had). She usually wore a white uniform cinched at the waist, or sometimes a pink one, with big pockets. And she always wore a girdle—girdles were the thing back then, way before Spanx—and she would always complain about it, saying it was too tight. After school, or when I was sick, we would watch game shows together. We loved *The Match Game, Password,* and *Hollywood Squares.*

We would also watch soap operas, or what she called "her shows."

"I have to watch my shows," she would say. *Search for Tomorrow, Days of Our Lives,* and *Another World.* Those were her "must-sees."

There was also another woman who would sometimes come and help clean. But Mrs. McCoy ran the house.

That is not to suggest that my mother wasn't perfectly capable of taking care of herself and the house, not to mention everyone else around her. She was not someone who was ever lounging around expecting other people to take care of her. Not at all! My mother was a do-er. Extra hands, to her, were just that—an extra pair of hands for her. And with her busy schedule, extra help was, well, helpful.

Yet my mother was totally capable of doing it all herself—cooking, cleaning, ironing, folding, tidying, vacuuming, and dusting. She actually enjoyed those things. She thought they were good exercise, too. Housework keeps you moving. It keeps you young. Keeps you vibrant. And it has an added benefit: You end up with a clean house.

She was also really good at thinking three steps ahead. She would often say to me that if you were leaving one room and going to another, you should think about whether there was something that needed to be taken to that vicinity. For example, if you were going upstairs, but you were going to pass the kitchen along the way, then you should see if there was anything that needed to be taken to the kitchen.

Always think ahead, she said. Be proactive. Don't just act.

That's a lesson that was harder for me to impart to my own kids. I always tended to think for them, feeling it was just easier for me to do it myself. So, if I were leaving a room, I would say to myself, "OK, I'm going to take along everything that I possibly can because nobody else is going to do it." I would do it all, and often, because of that, my kids didn't even think about taking anything themselves. It wouldn't even occur to them because I didn't teach it to them.

But it wasn't all about saving time and energy. Housekeeping chores were (and are) all good ways to keep the body fit. As a dancer, my mother was very much an athlete. She had to constantly keep her body working, and her mind as well. Something as simple as vacuuming could be used as a tool to keep your muscles and ligaments moving, and to keep all the synovial fluids flowing properly through the body.

That was something that applied not only to housework, but gardening as well. Yes, we also had gardeners, who tended to the property and kept it looking manicured and healthy. The many trees and plantings in and around our little enclave were more than one person could handle. So we relied on a German father and son who my mother admired and often sought out for "earthy" advice. We would sometimes go to their home, where the mother would make us a wonderful meal and they would share stories of their lives before coming to the U.S.

But my mother was very much hands-on when it came to the outdoors as well. She would be out there with her hands in the dirt just as much as anybody else. Connecting with the soil gave her tremendous joy.

No, she wouldn't actually mow the lawn herself. (She probably would have, but we lived in California; there wasn't much of a lawn to mow.) Yet she was always tending to the plants, moving bushes here and transplanting shrubs there. Whatever home she lived in, she always made sure that it had a huge garden. And because the vegetables that she grew were enough to feed an entire town, my mother often shared the harvest with everyone. She would go to the neighbors and give them extra corn, lettuce, and tomatoes, sometimes even cooking up the collard greens she had grown and delivering them along with the rest of the bounty.

She also didn't think it was necessary to spend money to be physically fit. If you want to weight train, she said, just pick up something heavy. Mostly, she believed it was important to be constantly moving—that the human body is supposed to always be in motion. Equally important was that you be limber. That meant that you not only had to do things to strengthen yourself, but also to stretch regularly to stay pliable.

As a little girl, there were only two people I saw who worked out on a regular basis: my mother and Jack LaLanne. That was it. Back then, Jack LaLanne—the fitness guru whose TV exercise show ran from 1951 all the way to 1985—was the only person anyone saw doing exercise. And my mother was like a female version of Jack LaLanne, even if people didn't think of her that way.

She didn't actually watch his show. But she didn't need to. She had her own way of adding fitness into her daily life. When we were in the vegetable garden, for example, she would say to me, "When you bend down to pick a head of lettuce, you plié." (This referred to a common dance move, now also known as a squat in fitness lingo.) Then she would demonstrate how to get the most possible mileage out of reaching down to pick a head of lettuce, or any of the other produce that we grew.

I learned in this way how to pick lettuce, as well as strawberries and all sorts of other fruits and berries. I also learned the proper way to release them from their stems. You don't just reach down and pull them off the plant. You have to detach them at a certain place, or you'll kill the roots of the plant. You want Nature to continue giving its bounty, and if you treat it properly, and take from it gently, then it will continue to replenish.

She would show me that when you bent down to pick that head of lettuce, or whatever else it might be, you didn't just lean over and grab it. You squatted, protecting your back and so that your legs got a workout, too. Who else ever thought about this, other than my mother . . . and maybe Jack LaLanne?

My mother was very deliberate about everything in that way. Sitting properly not only helped to strengthen your legs as you lowered yourself, but also kept your core tight when you sat correctly without slouching. And when you stood up, you didn't push yourself up with your arms. You used your legs again. No wonder she had such amazing legs.

So, as a little girl, I would often be running and jumping through the garden. And if I jumped off a higher surface, my mother would say to me, "Go back up there and do it again. You don't land like that, with your legs straight! That's not good for your back." When you jumped off something, you needed to bend your knees as you landed, to lessen the impact, she would say.

I now have that internalized. If I jump off something, I hear my mother's voice instantly.

I also hear it when I do a boot camp form of fitness training, which I sometimes do, along with yoga, to stay fit. Often these training sessions include "box jumps." Yep. They're exactly like it sounds. We jump on and off these boxes. Sometimes they are hard wooden boxes, and other times softer ones (which, after having missed the box a few times, my shins very much appreciate). When we do these, I almost always think that I'm the only one I know who was actually taught how to jump off a box and land like a graceful cat (although at times I feel more like an elephant, but that's for another day). Did *your* mother teach you how to jump off a box? Well, mine did.

One of her greatest sources of exercise by far, though, was her dogs.

Having connected so deeply with animals as a young girl, she always kept them around throughout her life. Dogs, mostly, but cats, too. If you went into her dressing room, there was always a dog or two lying on a piece of her clothing. To her, animals helped you stay active and gave you unconditional love on a level of which human beings were incapable. And that was really important to her. In our house in Los Angeles, I remember at one point having three or four dogs, along with who knows how many cats?

She had gotten our white standard poodle, Snowball, when I was born. He was incredibly smart, and my mother would tell me he was like my baby-sitter. She would seat me outside in the yard sometimes, and I'd be sleeping in the baby carriage. And she would tell Snowball, "Don't let anybody near her." I don't know who would possibly have come near me. We lived in the middle of nowhere. But she said he was the best guard dog ever. If anybody drove up to the gate, he would start growling and not let them near me.

She understood, though, as she got older, that pets don't just protect you and provide companionship. They can also give you the impetus to get off the couch and start moving. If you have a dog, then you have to take that dog out. Having a dog forced her to get up and out, even on the days when she might not have felt like doing it. For that reason, she saw having a pet as a means of keeping healthy. She also loved being outdoors, and if you had a dog, then you didn't need to go outside solo.

Her biggest secrets to staying fit and healthy, though, were about eating healthy food.

CHAPTER 22

Never Say Diet

There is a harvest whether we share with
a friend or a stranger.

To my mother, eating healthy wasn't a subject for negotiation. It was the rule. And not just in our house, but wherever and whenever eating, or even snacking, occurred. It wasn't about dieting or losing weight. Food was the body's fuel. And the kind of fuel you fill yourself with will result in the kind of body you end up with! Performance-wise, as well as with respect to appearance. Although my mother didn't ever diet, per se, she did eat like a bird. Small-sized portions, consumed slowly, just until she was full enough.

But she always ate full-fat everything—olive oil, butter, and whole milk—long before anyone had ever even heard of the Paleo or Keto plans. My mother only ate what she considered to be "real" food. If it didn't come from Nature, then she wouldn't put it in her mouth. I never saw her drink a soda. Certainly not a diet soda. Before it was chic to eat organic, my mother knew the importance of consuming pure, simple food. Fresh tomatoes, rice, sardines, a green leafy vegetable, and olive oil and garlic were all that she needed, and she was good to go.

She also drank her coffee with whole milk or cream. As I said, low-fat and nonfat were non-existent, as far as she was concerned. She understood that real butter, real milk, and real cream gave you more flavor. If you used just a little bit of them, you would be much more satiated than if you opted for the "fake" stuff. So, when my mother would cook up a plate of grits, it would be grits with butter, because margarine was just not on her radar.

Her travels also influenced her eating style. Since we spent a lot of time in Great Britain, she adopted some of its dietary habits. Kippers, for instance, a popular breakfast choice in London, were among her favorite things to eat. And if she couldn't find kippers, she would substitute a can of sardines and be in heaven. How she loved her sardines! Of course, being rich in calcium, selenium, and other essential nutrients, they are literally one of the healthiest things you can eat.

Personally, I must admit, I'm not a fan of sardines. I think they're vile. And I sure as hell wouldn't eat them straight out of the can. But my mother liked things simple, as well as conveniently packed. Peel back the lid on a can of sardines, add a hard-boiled egg and some salad, and you could feed her for the day.

Not one to frequent restaurants, as she preferred less fancy food to overly elaborate dishes, she would often travel with a rice cooker and use it to make rice or oatmeal in her hotel or dressing room. She wanted to be sure that she always had something healthy to eat, and she didn't want to depend on room service or catering.

Wherever we lived, my mother wanted to be able to grow her own food—unprocessed food grown without chemicals. So, whenever she moved to a new house, she always made sure that it had some land surrounding it. She may have cultivated a stage persona that longed for luxury, but offstage she was far more interested in cultivating crops. "As long as I have a piece of land," she would say, "I'll always have something to eat." She felt that if you had a little piece of land—even just a pot on a windowsill—then you could grow *something*. A tomato. Lettuce. Something that could nourish you.

And my mother loved to share her homegrown, nourishing food with friends, and with the cast and crew she was working with in the theater. She would often bring in food for everyone to enjoy, and much of the time she would also share the nutritional importance of the food she had prepared. "These are collard greens," she would say, "and this is how you should cook them. And this is why they're important to eat. . . ." (This was before collard greens were readily available in supermarkets, and they were still thought of as a Southern food.)

She had grown up with collard greens, and they remained one of her favorite things to cook. But these were not the Southern version known for being simmered for hours in fatback or lard with ham or pork. The ones my mother made were collard greens Eartha-style, sauteed in olive oil with onions and garlic. Simple preparation of food, she said, allowed "Nature's flavors" to really come through. And to be appreciated.

I think all mothers on some level are a bit stereotypical. They all want to give you food. Food is nourishment. Food is comfort. Food is home. But my mother wanted to give you REAL food. She touted the importance of eating string beans, zucchini, and kale, long before kale got a publicist and became popular. She also was conscious of how foods are better consumed in season. When she moved to the Northeast, the crops she chose to plant were slightly different from the ones she had grown in California, as she strongly believed in "eating local," another example of her being ahead of her time. She realized that because we Americans want our favorite foods year-round, store-bought produce is often shipped "before its time."

Healthy food, to my mother, wasn't limited to fruits and vegetables, though. She wasn't a vegetarian, even if fruits and veggies made up most of her diet. My mother always balanced her meals with some form of protein—the sardines I just mentioned, along with small amounts of meat and chicken (preferably grass-fed, if available). Or eggs.

We had ten or twelve chickens and two roosters in Beverly Hills, as well as doves. My mother loved the sound of doves!

We kept them all in an aviary that was the size of a New York City duplex apartment. It was huge. There were three levels to it. On the very top, in the back, were coops in which the chickens laid their eggs. The next two levels were just areas where they could wander around and hang out.

When my mother was home, she loved to go into the aviary and collect the eggs because she didn't really like to eat anything unless she knew where it had come from. So she would usually get the eggs herself. Yes, it was one of my chores to get the eggs, but those chickens and roosters and I did not get along. Whereas my mother had a connection to Nature and would walk into the aviary like Dr. Doolittle. Every creature would be cooing and clucking happily. And she would coo back or talk to them as if they understood each other.

Not me! When I would go in there, it was like the fox walking into the henhouse. The roosters would begin attacking me. The chickens would be screeching. The doves would fly around like crazy. And I would be yelling at them all. I didn't like being in there, any more than they liked having me. That was very well known by all concerned.

One of the main reasons I didn't like going into the aviary was because of those damn roosters. They were mean. I thought they were, anyway. They would charge toward me and try to peck at my legs. They weren't very nice. But, more importantly, I didn't want to eat those eggs.

I really hated those eggs. I wanted to eat the eggs my friends' parents bought at the supermarket instead. Eggs that were white and smooth. I didn't want the gross, brown ones with feathers on them, the ones that were all gunky! Sure, our eggs were much richer in flavor because our chickens weren't being fed any chemicals. But I didn't want to eat them, anyway. I wanted the nice, pristine eggs that came in cartons from the store. Not the ugly brown ones that our hens had laid, which were always warm and yucky. (Apologies if I have offended any chickens.)

We also had ducks. My mother loved duck eggs, too. She also loved taking care of . . . well, everything Nature gave birth to . . . the ducks, the chickens, the roosters, and the doves. What I loved was sitting outside the aviary and watching her do it. Tending to the fowl was not my cup of tea. As I got older, I would joke with her about it.

"You were born in the South on a cotton plantation," I would say, "and that is who you are. I was born in Beverly Hills. I'm supposed to be a princess. We do not *do* chickens and eggs and roosters and grow vegetables."

And she would always laugh and say, "What did I raise? How did I raise *you?*"

Of course, many people thought she was a little bit crazy, too. This was long before people became obsessed with organic food and eating healthy. There was no such thing as Whole Foods. There weren't best-selling books saying, "This is the way you should eat," or, "You need to grow your own vegetables." Unless you were from the country and you lived on a farm, you didn't think of doing that. Certainly not in the middle of Beverly Hills. My mother really was a Beverly Hillbilly.

At one point, however, the city came, and they took our chickens away. They actually confiscated the chickens because, they said, we weren't allowed to have them there. My mother wasn't about to stand for that, though. She went down to city hall and argued her point. She said that our property had been originally built as a stable, and that the aviary had always housed chickens, so ours should be grandfathered in.

My mother recalled this episode herself in her autobiography *Alone with Me*. "It wasn't long before the city tried to take my chickens away from me," she said. "One can't keep chickens in Beverly Hills, they told me. But I've never believed in the adage that you can't fight city hall. I collared the mayor and had heated discussions with him, and it was finally discovered that according to the statutes, any land that had housed livestock before 1954 was exempt from the ordinance prohibiting animals."

In the end, she was allowed to get her chickens back. OK, I don't know if she actually got her own chickens. But for years afterward, she would joke about how she had made a big stink about it. "I want the chickens that you took from me," she told them. "I don't want you giving me some other ratty old chickens! I want *my* chickens!"

We never ate any of those chickens, though. She wouldn't have been able to kill a chicken, or any other creature for its flesh. Quite the opposite. Remember the snails and slug story? She wouldn't have been able to kill any live thing herself. The chickens shared their eggs with us (although I'm not sure how voluntary that was), and then from the garden we got almost everything else. So my mother rarely needed to go to the store.

When she did go, though, you would not find her buying processed or precooked items. She would mostly stock up on staples such as rice, beans, coffee, and fresh breads, along with canned tuna and those much-loved sardines. Even when I was an infant, there was no prepared baby food for me. Nope. My mother would sometimes chew food up for me—like a bird does—and then feed it to me. Yes, that does sound gross; even as I write it, I am gagging just a little. Fortunately, I have no recollection of this. If I did, I would probably be in therapy for life. But, as necessity is the mother of invention, if she didn't have a blender nearby, then she would make her own baby food.

I also made baby food for my firstborn, but I used a food processor, not my teeth. Phew! Spared him that visual.

That reminds me of something crazy that happened when I was little.

I once ended up having to go to the doctor when we lived in Los Angeles because my teeth had turned orange. My mother never monitored my carrot intake. (I doubt that was even a thing.) So almost every time I walked past the garden, I would pick a fresh carrot and eat it. Turns out, when I was seven or eight, my teeth started to turn an interesting shade of orange or yellow. So, I guess, did my skin. But no one seemed to be able to figure out what was wrong with me.

Finally, one day I was sitting in the doctor's office and I had a carrot in my hand.

"How many carrots does she eat?" the doctor suddenly asked my mother.

"What are you talking about?" my mother replied. "I have no idea how many carrots she eats. We have a vegetable garden, and she goes and picks one whenever she wants to and eats it freely."

"Well, that may be the problem," he said. "I think she has carotene poisoning."

It had never occurred to my mother that you could get sick from eating vegetables. She felt that as long as you ate things that came out of the ground, and you knew what ground they had come from, then you would be healthy.

Eating fresh produce is not so easy to do when you live in a big city, of course (although Whole Foods and other organic or farmer's markets have now made that an issue of the past). My mother didn't consider living in an apartment to be a reasonable excuse for not planting something, though. You can live in an apartment and still have a tomato plant, she would say. She felt that people tend to make excuses for many things just because they don't want to do them. They make excuses to justify their laziness. At least she would call it laziness.

She always felt that eating junk food cost more in the long run than healthy eating. Eating properly, at least, didn't cost more than going out for fast food. Yes, you may be able to feed a family of four or more relatively cheaply at a fast-food restaurant. But the long-term effects of consuming a steady diet of fast food, on both the family and society, weren't worth the price, she felt, because of the health issues it could cause.

So she never understood why cities didn't encourage those group gardens (something that is thankfully beginning to change in more recent years). Maybe you could even turn these gardens into greenhouses, she believed, and grow tomatoes and other vegetables during the winter in the Northeast. That would help communities stay healthier, which would be more economical for everybody in the long run.

Obviously, one can't live on tomatoes alone. But feeding kids junk food—potato chips or "cola products," as she would call them—wasn't an option for her, either. I was never allowed to have anything like that. Believe me, I wanted it, though! I would have given my right arm for a bowl of Frosted Flakes. Or a Twinkie!

But the last thing my mother would ever have allowed me to have was junk food. It's no wonder that I still can't eat just one donut. Boy, do I love sweets! Whenever people ask me what my last meal would be, I say sixty-four Dunkin' Munchkins. Oh, yes, I would be able to eat every last one!

When something becomes taboo for you, no matter what it is—in my case, mainly any type of sweets, like cake or candy—then you crave that thing even more. I would go to my friends' houses and just want to sit by their snack drawer and savor every morsel of a Ding Dong (which are called Ring Dings in some areas), Pop-Tart, Twinkie, or Reese's Peanut Butter Cup until I was ready to explode (although I like to make the argument that the protein in peanut butter could qualify Reese's as a health food. Just sayin').

When it comes to food, I don't quite have my mother's sense of "balance." Sure, I understood her desire to be healthy, and to keep me healthy, too. But if she had allowed me to eat, say, a piece of home-made cake—a cake that maybe she would have baked herself, so that she knew what all of the ingredients were—as opposed to store-bought junk food, I think that would have provided a better balance for me than my being denied everything that other kids were allowed to eat.

In fact, even to this day, I cannot have just one bite of anything sweet. I'll sit and eat the entire bag. (One bag does mean one portion, right?) Fortunately, I'm blessed with a really good metabolism. I'm very lucky in that regard. I wish that I could do that thing where you eat clean and healthy all week, then have one day of eating almost anything that you want. But who wants to wait for that one cheat day?

I love the taste of food.

My mother was the exact opposite. She ate purely to exist. As I said, she ate very small portions. She didn't even qualify as a nibbler. But she didn't let her leftover food go to waste. On the occasions when she would go out to eat, she was known to carry empty Tupperware containers around in her purse. And if you were at her table—or any other table within her vicinity, for that matter—then any food that was left on a plate went into her Tupperware.

My mother had grown up in extreme poverty. She remembered what it was like to always be hungry. "You don't waste food!" she would say. "Nature didn't make it to be wasted."

Anything that wasn't fully consumed at home wasn't thrown into the garbage, either. Food scraps all went into the compost pile. Now, I know composting has become much more commonplace and "fashionable" these days. But when I was young, composting was not a thing. Certainly not in Beverly Hills, that's for sure. Nor were there cute little canisters into which you could toss your food remains that you could buy at Crate and Barrel and put on the kitchen counter. In our house, we had a makeshift garbage can in which my mother proudly stored vegetable and fruit peelings and uneaten leftovers until they were ready to be transported outside for composting. Quite embarrassing for a teenager, I might add.

It offended my mother to see people loading up their plates at all-you-can-eat buffets. Too often, she felt, much of what they had taken would end up sitting on their plates. "If you didn't want that much, then you shouldn't have taken it to begin with," she would say (silently most of the time). "Your eyes are always bigger than your stomach. Take only a small portion to start, and then, if you want more, you can always go back." That was her philosophy when it came to food.

This attitude also related to her generation. She was born in 1927. Soon after, there was the Great Depression, followed by World War II and other very difficult times. It wasn't just that my mother wasn't physically capable of eating a lot of food. I don't think she was mentally capable of it, either.

She carted around those plastic Tupperware containers for as long as I can remember. She carried them around knowing there was almost always going to be an opportunity to use them. If she went to a restaurant, then she knew she was prepared when the meal was over to collect whatever wasn't eaten, and she would say, "Now I have enough food for the next three days!"

Once again, always thinking ahead.

Now, if you were a regular Joe and you did things like that, then people would think you were just crazy. But when you're famous, as my mother was, then you have the luxury of being considered "eccentric" instead. So maybe heads turned, but most people held their tongues before questioning her behavior.

People find it quirky when famous people do unusual things. But as a daughter? It was embarrassing.

"Ma! Put that Tupperware back in your purse," I would exclaim. "We're in Le Cirque, for crying out loud! We're in one of the finest restaurants in the world!"

"So what?" she would snap back at me. "What does that matter? You still don't waste food! I don't care if I'm eating with the Queen of England. If she's going to leave a dinner roll on the table, then I'm going to see if she wants it. Waste not, want not!"

That was her attitude.

"You didn't grow up with no food," she would say to me. "You don't know what it's like to feel hungry."

She did. And she never forgot it. And maybe she never ate too much, in part, so that there was always something left over. So that she would never go hungry again.

CHAPTER 23

Pride and Prejudice

Blaze your trail. Beat to your own drum.

My mother deeply understood what it felt like to be mistreated and rejected. It was a pain that she was never able to let go of, and so she always did what she could to defend the underdog. She stood up, not just for people of color, but also the gay community, inner-city youth, all women, children, and anyone else whom she felt needed help. My mother understood the vital importance of "being heard." And when it came to standing up for others, for her it was not about donating money. She devoted her *time*.

There was one particular focus that she embraced with all her heart, though. My mother remembered the power that her teachers had had on her. How just a small amount of encouragement had dramatically changed her life's path. There were times when she even said that if she hadn't gone into show business, she probably would have been a teacher.

And so, starting when I was very young, my mother began teaching free dance classes for children in Watts, a low-income area of Los Angeles. In response to the terrible riots that took place there in 1965, she created a nonprofit organization called the Kittsville Youth Foundation. Although it was known as a dance and cultural arts program, it really had a much higher purpose. It was more about influencing a new generation, and encouraging young people—mainly Black, inner-city youths who didn't have many opportunities—to be proud of who they were.

The classes that my mother led there weren't about learning to dance, per se, as much as they were about movement. This was African movement, done to conga drums. My mother was very much about beat, sounds, and traditional African rhythms because she felt that rhythm is everywhere and was a fundamental part of how we experience our daily lives; that whatever people may listen to, whether it be the Beatles, country music, hard rock, or African music, we all hear a beat within ourselves. And that the African drums—that animalistic, raw, primitive sound—was how we had all started.

My mother also felt that everyone moved to a rhythm, and that we all needed to learn to listen to the beat within ourselves.

It's funny. I asked my husband, Allan, a year or so ago, "Do you have a song in your head all the time?" He said that he didn't. And I said, "Well, I always have some song or beat in my head." Sometimes it's obscure, and I don't know where I heard it. The other day, for example, I think it was something from *Mary Poppins*. Where I would have heard that, I have no idea. But I always have some type of music running in my head. Maybe I don't need the radio to be on because I have my own channel playing. Sometimes I wonder where all these songs come from. Where am I picking them up? What sparks an idea that starts that song in my head?

I am always aware that I seem to be moving rhythmically (clearly, my mother's impact), and that movement usually goes to the rhythm of whatever song is playing in my head. I'm always dancing or moving around, almost as if there are short-lived musicals occurring inside me daily. I remember my mother saying something very similar; that she was always listening to the sounds when she was living with her aunt in Harlem. She said that she grew up listening to the sounds of the street, and that there was always music playing there. "You moved to a rhythm," she would say.

I look at people now in New York City walking down the street, or when I'm on the subway or the train. So many of them walk around with headphones on, drowning out the city's sounds. I don't like to have headphones on myself because it makes me feel vulnerable. But I also think about what so many of these people are missing. How the energy of the hustle and bustle can feel. There are always so many cool sounds all around us. There are so many interesting things happening! Even outside of a big city.

My mother said, "Listen to the sounds of Nature, as well as her silence." The power of both is great.

My mother's Kittsville program helped teach young people to listen and tap into that energy. To appreciate the influence of loudness, as well as the strength of silence.

When she would teach these classes, which were open to children ages seven to eighteen, she always started by dancing to a rhythm. She would lead by moving across the floor of the gymnasium or dance studio, and then the kids would follow her, row by row. For her, it was less about learning a dance move, though, than connecting to your inner beat and learning how to carry yourself.

"How you present yourself to the world is crucial," she would say to them. "Look people in the eye, always hold your head up high, and when you walk into a room, feel a connection in your torso. Deep inside your gut. And be proud! You are unique, and you should shine."

As for manners? Well, we know how important those were to her. She required the kids who came to her classes to be well-behaved and to learn the importance of not only showing respect to the adults who were in attendance but to each other as well. She expected to be greeted with the words "Hello, Miss Kitt," accompanied by a firm handshake and direct eye-to-eye connection. Then she would have everyone sit down in a circle and she would talk to them.

"When you enter a room, walk in with pride," she would say. "Pull your shoulders back, dress properly, and speak clearly, saying, 'Yes, ma'am,' and 'No, ma'am,' because it's important to respect your elders. When you feel pride in yourself and you show respect, people take notice."

When you do all of those things, she told them, you are going to be treated very differently than you would if you shuffled in with your shoulders down and you mumbled, "Hey, how ya doin'?"

It made my mother cringe that many children weren't taught proper manners. "Manners matter!" she would say. Because when you carry yourself with pride, it makes you feel better about yourself. And when you feel better about yourself, then you project more confidence. And whether or not you get the job that you wanted, you still are able to walk out with your head held high, because you didn't lose it just because you didn't conduct yourself with pride and proper etiquette.

Language was also really important, she would tell the kids. The proper way to speak, and the proper way to enunciate. Mumbling, she would say, reflected poorly on a person and was not acceptable. Ditto to swallowing words or failing to pronounce all of the letters. My mother's longtime assistant, Jaki, was from Scotland, and she had a very heavy Scottish accent, and you couldn't hear her pronounce the letter "T." My mother would laugh sometimes and ask her, "Jaki, what *do* you do with your T's?"

She would speak to them about how crucial it was to surround yourself with the right kinds of people, too. It was essential to avoid bad influences, she said. She also encouraged her students to have good nutrition and to avoid junk food (big surprise!), and to take pride in their appearance. This had nothing to do with fashion or trends or wearing fancy clothes. It was entirely about putting your-self together to look respectable.

"Tuck your shirt in, don't ever wear your pants with your underwear showing, and always be as neat and clean as you can be," she said.

Over the decades that she taught there, countless youngsters heard this advice.

But my mother's wisdom was not restricted to the students who took her classes. She imparted it to almost everyone with whom she came in contact. Whether you were in a company she performed in or seated beside her at an event, you got her message.

Her Kittsville program started in the mid '60s, and she continued teaching in it into the early 2000s. She wanted to give kids a place to go after school and something to look forward to. And she did. Kittsville remains in existence to this day.

CHAPTER 24

A Star with Stage Fright

My flaws make me who I am.

My mother recalled having once been asked during a radio interview, "Is it true that when you wake up in the morning, you put your feet into mink-lined slippers, step over seven men, and brush your teeth with Dom Perignon champagne?"

"Yes, doesn't everybody?" was her playful, teasing reply. But that sort of talk was just part of her stage persona. She could be intimidating to people because she sang songs like "I Want to Be Evil" so convincingly. Yet as strong and confident as she appeared to be, that was not the whole story. My mother was actually quite shy.

What you would probably never guess, given the presence that she projected onstage, was that she also had terrible stage fright. Each time she would step onto the stage, it was as if it were for the very first time. In those few minutes, right before she went on, she needed total silence. She didn't want to be spoken to. Not one word.

She needed a moment.

It didn't make any difference that she had been performing for years. Every time felt new to her. She had a genuine fear that nobody was going to show up. That the seats would be empty. That the audience wasn't going to accept her. Or that they weren't going to like her.

Those childhood fears, which were always close at hand, would rear their ugly heads when she was at her most vulnerable. Alone. On that stage. There were no back-up singers. No special guests. No one sharing the stage with her beyond members of her band. Talk about being exposed!

The nerves would kick in when she would leave her dressing room and she was waiting in the wings. But they didn't last long. As soon as she took that first step onto the stage, and the spotlight hit her, she could feel the embrace of the audience, and it was as if she grew a few inches in that instant, as confidence and strength filled her body.

Before that, though, in the hours right before a performance, there were many things that had to be done behind the scenes.

Prep work.

Obviously, she had to get dressed in one of her many form-fitting gowns, which were often slit way up the side—not only to reveal her well-toned legs, but to allow her to showcase her natural grace and dancer's training.

Offstage, though, my mother was much more comfortable ditching the glamour. Sweatpants, T-shirts, and sweatshirts were much more her style. She didn't want to bring attention to herself when she was out casually in public. Dressing like that was, in part, her attempt to remain incognito. I always thought that was funny, because she would wear these oversized dark glasses and this big hat, which usually only managed to bring her more attention.

"Mom," I would say, "you are not hiding behind that hat!" And, of course, with her unmistakable voice, her identity was always known the minute she uttered a word.

If she wasn't performing, she would never wear makeup, either. Not a stitch of it. She preferred to let her skin breathe when she could, since stage makeup can be very heavy. As for her hair, it was almost always in a scarf when she wasn't performing because she wore wigs when onstage. Her natural hair was hardly ever seen in public, unless she had it pulled back.

Her hair had been long before I was born, but from all the years of wearing wigs it had started to break off, which was frustrating for her, so she kept it short. If she went out at night, she would usually just tie it up in a silk scarf like a turban. She had the same makeup artist for at least fifteen years, Carlo Geraci, and he did both her hair and makeup. He often traveled with us. If she was doing a Broadway show, or appearing in concert close to home, then he would come to her late in the afternoon and stay until midnight, or whenever she was done.

Carlo and I referred to each other as Lucy and Ethel. We had the most fun together! Giggling and laughing at situations we found amusing, like two little kids misbehaving in church. My mother sometimes found this annoying, and she would get angry at him—not seriously angry, just testy—and, taking advantage of the situation, I would make fun of that. That, of course, would make her testy with me, and then he would make fun of *that*. We thought we were hysterical. In this way, we would play off each other. He was like a second child to her.

For each performance, my mother wore these special dressing covers. They weren't dressing gowns, exactly, more like capes, thrown over her shoulders to help her stay warm on her way to the stage, in case she would pass through air-conditioning. My mother was very vulnerable to bronchitis, and to feeling cold, so she needed to stay covered right up until she would make her entrance. So we would have these special robes custom-made to match her gowns. My mother always preferred to wear clothes that were coordinated, even if that particular piece wasn't going to be seen in public.

Sipping hot tea with lemon and sucking on one of those Fisherman's Friend lozenges were also part of her pre-stage rituals. But she had to spit the lozenge out before she went onstage, which meant that you would have to have a tissue for her. And if you didn't have a tissue handy, then it often went into your bare hand.

Usually my bare hand.

None of this was complicated, of course, but my mother was very meticulous. In those last few minutes, to help with her nerves, you had to make sure that she had all of the things she needed before she went onstage.

All of this was not unusual for a singer. Many performers have their "game day" rituals, athletes and artists alike. These rituals don't necessarily have anything to do with superstition. They are often just habits that gradually grow into needs—needs that many people, including my mother, find comfort in and come to rely on as they begin their process of preparation. For my mother, this prep work would also include vocal exercises that she would do inside her dressing room to warm up her throat. These were often common tongue-twisters, but hers always had a special Eartha twist.

My mother thought that tongue-twisters helped keep her mind alert and loosened the muscles in her mouth so that the words could come out "trippingly off the tongue." And I'm not talking about the usual ones, like Peter Piper and his peck of pickled peppers. One of her favorite tongue-twisters, which she did in one breath, went like this: "Betty Botter bought some butter. But, said she, 'This butter's bitter. If I put it in my batter, it will make my batter bitter.' So she bought a bit of butter that was better than the bitter butter, so 'twas better Betty Botter bought a bit of better butter." Give that one a try!

Proper enunciation, as I have said, was very important to my mother, so starting when I was very little, we would practice saying that one together, and others like it. Clear speech and a quick mind—those were two essential qualities to possess. So she made learning these word puzzles fun and often included them in my bedtime routine.

What she was doing for herself was practicing breath control, as she would try to recite the Betty Botter tongue-twister twice in one breath, which is a lot. As a young singer, she had learned the importance of breathing from your diaphragm, not your chest, and of not speaking nasally. She understood the science behind how the human body functioned when she was performing and embraced the athleticism needed to keep her on her A game.

She didn't make many demands in her contracts, though. She wasn't diva-esque. But she did have certain requirements. For instance, she didn't want a stage with carpeting because carpets not only limited freedom of movement, but could also be a cause of injury if the heel of her shoe got caught. She also requested that a wooden stage not be waxed, which was for practical reasons, too. She had once fallen on a slippery stage early in her career and fractured one of her ribs.

When you hear stories about celebrities who demand that dressing rooms be painted a certain color for them, or that they need a certain type of straw to drink from, or they will eat only one color of M&Ms (yes, that is a thing). . . . Well, that definitely was not my mother.

But she did also have certain necessary rituals for after a performance. These mostly involved fans, who would gather at the stage door. It was very important to my mother that she make herself available to sign autographs for anyone who took the time to wait for her after a show.

When she came off the stage, it could take a while for her to come down from that "stage high." Removing the costumes, wigs, and then finally the makeup, she would start to shed the Eartha Kitt persona, getting closer to being Eartha Mae again as each layer was peeled away. When she emerged to sign autographs, no longer wearing her costumes and high heels, many fans were surprised by how tiny she was. This contributed to her sense of vulnerability, as most people towered over her. If they came in close and surrounded her, it could be a bit disturbing and unnerving for her because she was so petite.

But she would stand out there anyway and autograph every single program, or picture, or whatever else people brought her to sign. People were often surprised by how long she would stay to sign and take photos. But it never occurred to her to do it any differently. It never crossed her mind to *not* be there for them. Those fans had stood out there for her. They had paid for their tickets. They had gone out of their way. The least she could do was go out of hers. The woman who was sometimes afraid that the seats would be empty was going to make sure that she showed her appreciation in kind.

Sometimes she was tired. Really tired. But she understood that even if you're tired, connecting with people gives you adrenalin, and the serotonin that gets fed by feeling appreciated and wanted. This was the positive feedback that that little urchin Eartha Mae still yearned for. My mother understood the importance of those moments. And that, even if it was impossible to make up for the years of wanting, her fans helped fill that massive void.

Sometimes she would get into the car afterward and literally collapse. "I'm exhausted! So exhausted," she would say. Even so, she would stay out there until the last person left. It didn't matter how late it was, or how weary she might be. Her fans, to her, were her family. Usually, one of her assistants would be with her, and very often that was me. There would also be a driver waiting for her. She was never left alone because, as I said, she was very small and felt vulnerable in large crowds.

But there was one thing that was absolutely essential after a show: If you worked for my mother, then you had better have a Sharpie pen on your person. She only liked to sign autographs with Sharpies. And having more than one on hand was imperative, because Sharpies sometimes dry up. If you didn't have a Sharpie, or preferably two, and she needed one, then you would get the stare of death.

Which could actually be pretty funny sometimes. Her other support staffers and I would laugh about it and make fun of each other, pointing fingers at the perceived culprit.

"*He* was supposed to have the pens," I would say about Carlo.

"No, *she* was!" he would say, causing us both to receive the death stare from her. My mother was able to also see the humor once we were in the car and on the way home.

Then there was the time that I did have a Sharpie after the show. But what my mother really seemed to want was something even sharper.

CHAPTER 25

An Unwelcome Blast from the Past

I am never afraid of memories;
they remind me of who I am.

One night, after my mother performed at Carnegie Hall, we came out through the stage door. I was standing beside her, watching her begin to sign autographs, when a woman in the crowd began to yell, "Eartha! Eartha Mae! It's me!"

My mother didn't respond. I kept tugging at her arm, saying, "Mom, I think that woman is trying to get your attention." I knew that my mother had heard her, but she kept pretending that she hadn't. She just kept signing autographs, completely ignoring her. Finally, the woman said, "Don't you remember me?"

Then she said her name.

That, my mother heard. It was a name that she recognized from her childhood in South Carolina. It stopped her right in her tracks, and she was suddenly frozen in time. In an instant, she had been transported back to being that little toddler who had been abandoned by her mother. The look on her face changed completely as she turned, and froze, and clearly started to unravel as she lunged toward the woman, filled with a lifetime of tears, anger, and rage.

I had never seen my mother lose control like that. She never really got upset or acted hastily. She was always so calm and deliberate. So to see her become unnerved by what was to me a complete stranger took me, as well as everyone else around her, by surprise.

I forcefully grabbed hold of her and rushed her into the waiting car, and we quickly drove away. By now she was shaking and crying. "I never knew how I would react if I ever came face to face with someone from my childhood," she said. "Now I know."

She knew exactly who that woman was. I'm not sure she would have recognized her by sight alone after so many years. But the moment this woman had said her name, my mother had known, and remembered.

She also knew who she herself was—that beneath all of the fame and success, she was still that cotton picker from the South who had grown up poor, hungry, abused, and rejected.

She was Eartha Mae.

There were two different personas that coexisted inside my mother. She would even refer to them differently. "That's Eartha Kitt," she would say, "and this is Eartha Mae."

They were both authentic and both very much a part of each other all the time. One would just take precedence over the other whenever it was imperative to do that. The Eartha who came out whenever she stepped onto the stage was Eartha Kitt.

Eartha Kitt gave my mother the fearlessness it took to stand on a stage in front of a crowd of strangers and sing or act, because I think doing that takes a lot of guts.

Yet no matter how far she had come, Eartha Mae always remained at the core of Eartha Kitt. Eartha Kitt had been built on that foundation. My mother never let go of that pain, in part because she didn't want to. She wanted to remember who she was and where she was from.

She would use it to her advantage, keeping it under her control. Not only did it help her relate to song lyrics and characters that she might play when she was working, but it was why she always felt compelled to LISTEN when people would share their life stories with her. The pain from her past was always there right beneath the surface.

"Why would you want to hold on to something that's so painful? That's toxic?" I would ask her.

And she would say, "I don't think that pain is toxic. It's WHO I am! It's a part of me." Her having coined the phrase, "I have taken all of the manure that has been thrown at me all my life and used it as fertilizer" couldn't have been more spot on!

Back in 1954, she had starred in *Mrs. Patterson* on Broadway, portraying a young Black woman in the South who dreams of being wealthy. Summoning the pain that she still felt inside had made that character a little too real for my mother. When the play opened to stellar reviews, those memories made her feel uncomfortable and unworthy of her success.

"Eartha Kitt was being accepted in the civilized world of luxury and comfort, but could Eartha Mae be accepted also?" she later wrote. "Eartha Mae is a child of the dirt, she knows how to survive there, she knows poverty and rejection. She thinks once given away she will always be given away."

That continuing fear of rejection was often hard for my mother to quiet inside herself. Eartha Mae had a way of rising to the surface unexpectedly, as she had, to the extreme, that night after the show at Carnegie Hall. When that would happen, my mother felt worthless and rejected all over again. Despite all of her success, she continued to struggle with the feeling that she didn't really belong.

When this woman hit that one raw place, my mother tried to ignore it because she could feel that if she went there, then the dam was going to break. Plus, the woman had called her "Eartha Mae." And hearing someone other than herself refer to her that way was destabilizing. Eartha Mae had to be protected. She was a tiny little girl who was hurt and scared. She had been abandoned and rejected and abused. She had been left alone with no one to care for her.

I look back now and try to imagine how my mother must have felt as a little girl, and how frightening life must have been for her. How can emotions like that not stay with you forever, and mold who you become?

As an adult, she must have looked back and wondered how it was possible for people to know that this little girl was being treated so badly and not do anything about it. Why hadn't someone come to her aid? Children, after all, are helpless, unable to get themselves out of difficult or dangerous situations. Why had no one been willing to speak up on her behalf?

Even so, that woman at the stage door had been just a child at the time herself. She'd had no power to do anything on my mother's behalf. The truth was that even the adults around her probably hadn't had much power, either. It's hard to talk logically, though, to someone who feels that level of hurt.

"Let go of that already!" I would tell her. "That's old stuff!" But I might as well have been pleading with a wall. It was never going to happen with my mother. No matter how far she went in life, she carried those scars of rejection inside her.

She had left the South so many years earlier, in the 1930s. She had left behind the people but not the memories. And because of that, she never felt the need to "find her family." There were people who contacted her from time to time, claiming that they were relatives. But after I was born, she would often look at me and say, "My only family is sitting right here. *This* is my family. I don't have or need anyone else."

She wasn't bitter, per se. But when she talked about the South—and mostly about the adults who had abused her—she did not speak of it fondly. I guess you could say that maybe there was bitterness, and anger. Albeit justified.

She would often comment that mistreating a child was like kicking a dog—an innocent creature that needs an adult to care for them. And in this case, the child who had been mistreated was *her*. My mother used to say to me, "Pay attention to how people treat animals. Because if they will mistreat an animal, then you can rest assured that, on some level, they will do the same to a person."

Still, that troubling incident at Carnegie Hall was out of character for her. I kept watching her body language and her face because I knew she had heard that woman. You could almost see a movie camera with the reel going backward, faster and faster, all the way back to that cotton plantation and the little girl she had once been. Those emotions and her response were that little girl screaming in pain.

"Don't panic." That's what my mother had always said to me. Even in times of peril, like an earthquake, or a car accident, she never panicked herself. I had never seen her hysterical like that. So to witness the intense response she had was unnerving for me. It was like that woman had managed to unleash the one little part of my mother that she had kept buried for so long. This woman had pricked her, like the needle had pricked Sleeping Beauty's finger, and that was that. Except in this case, it didn't make her fall asleep. Rather, the rage hidden inside her had suddenly woken up.

Usually, she was able to keep it under wraps, drawing from it as she needed to by turning to those memories—the really raw part—and using them as "fertilizer," keeping her on a path and forging ahead. The Eartha Mae in her had remained inside. Until that moment.

CHAPTER 26

Go East, Young Woman

*Trust your instincts. They will always put you
on the right path.*

Finally, after a decade, my mother's days on the blacklist were over. In 1978, she appeared on Broadway again, in *Timbuktu!*, a show based on the musical *Kismet*, with an all-Black cast. Famed dancer and actor Geoffrey Holder was not only directing, but also doing the costumes and choreography, and he chose her to play one of the leads, Sahleem-La-Lume. That was the part Marlene Dietrich had played in the original 1944 movie. The show was a huge hit, and the role would garner her a second Tony nomination, for Best Actress in a Musical.

But just as important, she would often talk about the feeling she had the moment she first stepped back onto that Broadway stage. The audience broke into show-stopping applause, and she knew, in that instant, that her path had brought her back again, and that she was home to stay.

The show opened at the Ford Theatre in Washington, D.C. President Jimmy Carter invited her to the White House and personally welcomed her there. It was a far cry from her last visit to the White House, and another heartwarming sign that she was indeed *home.*

But after three months, the show moved to New York, meaning that our home would have to be there now. I was only seventeen at the time and a senior in high school—not exactly the ideal time to relocate. But I was still at the Lycée Francais, a school frequently attended by diplomats' children, meaning they were used to having kids coming in and out all the time. (The Lycée was a really small school at the time. It remains small to this day, albeit with added campuses, but then it was so small that there may have been only 30 kids in my class.)

It looked like my mother was going to be in New York for a long time, and then the show was going to go on the road after its Broadway run. I didn't feel like I had any reason to stay in California. There was really nothing there for me if my mother wasn't there. So I went East with her.

I had been to New York many times, but I had never actually lived there. The biggest city I had ever lived in was London. (It's hard for me to consider Los Angeles to really be a city because it's so spread out.)

Moving to New York was a new adventure. We sublet an apartment on 57th Street and Park Avenue, on the 51st floor of a big, modern apartment building. Talk about a lifestyle change! Living high up, almost in the clouds, looking down on the hustle and bustle of the city, learning how to hail a taxi, navigating through so many people just to get around, was quite the learning curve for me. There were certainly no chickens or vegetable gardens there.

My mother soon began rehearsals, and I finished high school remotely with some tutoring help, then started taking a few classes at Hunter College. By the time my mother went on tour with *Timbuktu!*, I was starting to settle into a routine and making new friends, so I stayed in New York. One day, the friend of my mother's who had sublet her apartment to us came back for a couple of days. She was a producer and was there to hold backers' auditions for a new Broadway show. I remember Stephen Sondheim sitting at the piano in the living room singing for potential investors for something called *Sweeney Todd.*

I was in the bedroom listening to the songs, and I also overheard the plot. "This is the worst idea ever!" I remember thinking. "Who would go see a show about a crazed barber who kills people and grinds up their bodies to put in mincemeat pies? This is horrific!" That just shows you how much I knew. Good thing that I wasn't a potential producer. I saw it when it opened on Broadway, with Angela Lansbury and Len Cariou. It won eight Tony Awards in 1979, including best musical, and it was amazing!

Soon after we moved to New York, I also started modeling a bit.

I first signed with Click Models, then with Bethann Management, an agency run by Bethann Hardison, a Black supermodel who broke barriers in the '70s by appearing in major magazines like *Harper's Bazaar* and *Vogue*. But I ended up mostly doing catalog shots for department stores. This was at the point at which fashion models were starting to top six feet. And at five-foot-eight, I was relatively tall, but not exactly gargantuan. Yes, there were still some models back then who were my height, but they were growing much taller by then, and I had clearly reached my maximum height.

I hadn't really had much direction, career-wise, in my life. After all, I had a mother who said I was great at everything I did. Good for the ego, but not so helpful for focusing on a specific path. So modeling seemed to make sense.

I liked doing it at the time, but modeling can be a very difficult industry. It's tough to be judged strictly on your looks. It doesn't matter what you sound like, or who you are as a person, or the level of your intellect. It's all about what you look like and how photogenic you are.

It helped that I had been raised by a woman who gave me a great deal of self-esteem, but it's an industry that will absolutely destroy you if you don't have thick skin. Thankfully, it didn't tear me down. I'm one of those people who are like the Energizer Bunny. It's hard to beat me down.

I continued modeling for about eight years—probably longer than I should have. I was never particularly successful at it, though. In college, you don't have classes all day long, so you're free to attend "go-sees" and do all the rest of the things that you need to do, especially if you're living in New York City, as I was.

I also began to dabble at that point in the entertainment business. I auditioned for some commercials, as well as a couple of TV shows. I did a few commercials, including one for a shopping mall, although nothing all that earth-shattering. I later auditioned for a daytime soap and actually got screen-tested. But it came down to me and another person, and you can probably guess what the outcome was. That's the nature of the business.

I also auditioned for some movies, and once read for one with Bill Cosby, with whom my mother had appeared in 1965 on the TV show *I Spy*, a role for which she was nominated for her first Emmy (in 1966, for Outstanding Single Performance by an Actress in a Leading Role). I don't think that movie ever got made, but let's just say there was no love lost between them. I recall him saying to me at the time, "If you get this role, I don't want your mother on the set."

And I told him, "Don't worry. She doesn't *want* to be on the set."

(I don't know what went down between them during the filming of *I Spy*. I'll just say that I don't think she would be surprised by all of the allegations against him.)

But I was reluctant to try to compete with my mother, so I never pushed for a career in the entertainment industry with any real vim and vigor. I'm not sure if I was afraid that I would be compared to her, and that people would say, "You're not as good as your mother." Or, on the contrary, they would have said, "You're even better!" And then where would that have left her? Neither result would have been a great outcome, and I guess I didn't want to risk finding out.

Instead, the following year, I enrolled at Barnard College, the women's liberal arts college associated with Columbia University. I didn't live in the dorms, though. I lived at home. Or, to be accurate, in an apartment located in the same building as my mother's. (I know, what a risk taker I was.)

That meant that I didn't quite have a normal college experience, or anything like it, for that matter. I commuted. It was a bit like going to high school. I would get on the bus, or sometimes I'd drive to school. Yes, I actually had a car in New York City, because, well, I was a California girl. Never mind that we lived in New York now. I was still going to drive everywhere.

Plus, you know, it was college. You go for one class, or maybe two. Then you go home. At that point, I didn't live with my mother, however. I had my own place.

My mother had taken two apartments on East 87th Street, on the 29th floor of a building, and she had turned them into one giant apartment. Why we needed all that space, I'll never know. It was huge! That was just silliness, as far as I was concerned, because it was only for my mother and me . . . and the animals, of course—a dog and a cat and a bird.

She lived in that giant place for a long time, but I soon moved out. Out to the eleventh floor, that is. Most kids go away to college. Moving downstairs was as far as I ever went myself. I still felt like Miss Independent, though. And it actually worked really well.

It was a studio apartment, in the same building as my mother, yes, but I rarely saw her. She was not one to just drop in. We just talked on the phone a lot, which was hysterical. We might as well have had an intercom. She had rented this apartment for me, and I lived there with my black cat named Kizzy.

For the average kid, the biggest part of the college experience may be leaving home, but not for me. It wasn't that my mother wouldn't have allowed me to live elsewhere. I think I just wanted to live in my own apartment more than I wanted to live on campus. I wasn't yearning for the typical college experience. Maybe because of all the traveling and moving around I had done as a kid, I didn't feel the need to have that.

Also, on some level, whether I was conscious of it or not, my being present or available at all times to give my mother an anchor was very important. Important for both of us. If I had really wanted to have more distance from her, I probably could have. But I didn't want to, so it never came up. Being 18 floors away from her seemed like the perfect solution. Living on campus had no appeal to me. I'm not really sure why. I guess I didn't know anybody. And I didn't really *care* to know anybody. I was much happier going back to my own apartment than I was interested in hanging out. I wasn't a party person. I didn't drink, as I said, and didn't do drugs. I wasn't a goofy teenager. I was much more of an adult in many ways, but not the typical young adult—a serious adult.

My mother also was on tour a lot, so she wasn't necessarily even there. But I didn't ever feel lonely. I made a couple of good friends at school, and we were really, really close. But I was still more comfortable being in my own space than living in a college dorm. I would spend time with other kids at school, then go back to my own base. Even as a kid, I had always preferred to be in my own space, and never really had sleep-overs at friends' houses.

I was always pretty much a loner. Just as my mother was. I liked being by myself. I liked my own company. Still do.

I guess you could say that, as outgoing as I may seem, I'm really an introvert, and my mother was definitely an introvert, too. As much as she adored her fans, and was infinitely grateful to them for their support, she felt that people drained the energy out of her. Sometimes that happened in a good way, but it still depleted her to be around other people all the time. And I guess I feel that way, too. I'm happy being alone.

I know a lot of people who are not comfortable with that. Spending time with just themselves. Obviously, my growing up as an only child contributed to that. Only children often learn to entertain themselves because they have to. But I have found that being alone—without the need to make conversation or be distracted by anyone else—is not only a positive trait to possess, but has also taught me to be self-sufficient, self-reliant, and comfortable in my own skin.

That is not to say I was always alone back then, though, mind you. I didn't just have those good friends. I dated, and I even had some boyfriends . . . some of whom my mother actually liked.

The truth was, though, that she hadn't made romantic relation-ships a priority in her own life for many years by then. If anything, she was wary of getting into another relationship. I don't think she had been particularly wary of my getting into a romantic relation-ship. But then, as I got older, that changed.

ABOVE: Meeting a new friend in Australia. BELOW: A holiday dinner at our home in Beverly Hills. Guess I was questioning the menu.

Piggyback rides are
often necessary.

I adored my
Grandma Nora.

ABOVE: We always had fun together.
BELOW: Our return to the amusement park in Durban, South Africa.

ABOVE AND BELOW: My mother leading classes at Kittsville Youth Foundation, the cultural arts and dance program she created for inner-city kids in LA.

RIGHT: The little stuffed fox I found in that Vienna church still sits on a shelf in my closet. BELOW: Offstage, my mother favored casual clothes with her hair usually tied up in a scarf.

ABOVE: My mother serenading the chickens. She could even mesmerize a rooster.
BELOW: My mother loved living near water.

There was always time for a hug, no matter how big I got.

Sometimes we went out. (Yes, I am wearing two watches.)

ABOVE: My mother and Rachel walking her dogs in NYC. BELOW: A contemplative moment between "Nana" and Rachel at my mother's house in Connecticut.

My mother with Rachel and Jason.

With Allan on our wedding day.

My wedding day with Allan and all of our kids.
(Left to right: Allan, Rachel, my mother, Eric, Nicole, me, and Jason)

ABOVE: Even during "down time," my mother always stayed busy.
BELOW: One of my mother's many needlepointed "masterpieces."

RIGHT: I told you I love donuts.
BELOW: One of the many things
my mother taught me was to never
take yourself too seriously.

ABOVE: Guess it was "Dress in Red and Blue Day."
BELOW: Allan and me with our blended family (left to right: Eric, Nicole, Rachel, and Jason).

CHAPTER 27

Workouts and Wedding Bells

*No one has less to live for than one
who lives for himself alone.*

A year or two after I left Barnard, my mother bought a house in New Milford, Connecticut. It had eighty-seven acres of land and had been built in 1773. It was a pretty cool place that my mother completely renovated to expose its original and historic beauty. But I was young and single, and—no offense to New Milford, Connecticut—I didn't want to live there. So I stayed in New York.

I lived on the West Side for a year, then moved to the East Side for another year, to a building on East 72nd Street, right across from Sotheby's.

There was a health club in my building, and I would work out in it all the time. I was really serious about my workouts, so I wouldn't frequent the gym when lots of other people were there. I had no interest in socializing or making small talk. I just wanted to work out by myself, then go back to my apartment. One of my girlfriends kept saying, "You're never going to meet anybody this way. You've got to leave your apartment!"

My friend was older than I was and was preoccupied with my meeting a man. She felt that you are not complete without a "significant other." But, personally, I was perfectly content being alone.

"No, I'm fine," I would tell her.

Meet someone or not meet someone? That just wasn't on my radar. So I would work out at nine at night, right before the gym closed. I preferred to have the place all to myself.

I didn't have it quite all to myself, though. There was this guy who was always working out at the same time. He wore old scrubs, or what looked to me like scrubs. We never spoke to each other, however. Like me, he was entirely focused on working out. Then one day I was having a conversation with the woman at the desk, and he was talking to her, too. Finally, she said, "You guys need to meet. You're always here at the same time and never acknowledge each other's existence. Kitt, this is Charles Shapiro. Charles, this is Kitt."

Now we knew each other's names, so every time we saw each other, we would say hello and chat a little. And before long, we weren't just engaging in conversation. We were engaged to be married.

"See?" I said to my friend. "Guess I didn't have to leave my apartment, or at least my apartment building, did I?"

Of course, he ended up not being a doctor, after all. Charles was a lawyer. Why he was wearing those scrubs to work out, I never really understood.

We remained engaged for about a year and a half because I wanted to have a June wedding. I had seen Princess Diana walk down the aisle in her giant, poofy dress just a few years earlier, and that's what I wanted—to get married like the princess that I had been raised to think I was (yes, eye rolls are expected here). And so I got married at the Pierre Hotel, in a big poofy dress with a very long lace train and big shoulder pads. This was in 1987. It had to have shoulder pads.

I was only twenty-five at the time. Now, as the mother of a twenty-five-year-old daughter myself, I think that was a very young age at which to be married. My mother must have felt the same way about me. But at the time I felt that I was ready to be married, and I wanted a big, dreamy wedding.

My mother didn't see the need for that, though. After all, she had been married in a small civil ceremony in the living room of her house. She kept saying to me, "I'll give you a big wedding, if that's what you really want, but I think it's a total waste of money. Spend all that for a four-hour party? Why don't you just get married in Central Park?"

That was crazy talk in my mind! "I don't want to get married in a park!" I said. "I want a big, fancy Pierre Hotel wedding." And so that is what my mother gave me. And that is what she paid for— two hundred guests. She kept saying, "Where is it written that the bride's family pays for everything?"

My father couldn't afford to contribute. Not that my mother would have asked him to. She knew that I wanted him to be there, but *she* certainly didn't feel the same way. I think that when you're a little girl, you fantasize about having your father walk you down the aisle someday. At least I did. But when I got older, I realized what a slap in the face it would have been to my mother if I had allowed that to happen.

She was the one who had been there for me all those years. She was the one who had taken care of me, showered me with unconditional (although sometimes conditional) love. So I had my mother walk me down the aisle alone. My father only came as a guest.

My mother still tried hard to talk me out of spending all that money on the wedding. It wasn't that she didn't want me to get married. Well . . . she did and she didn't. She did because she wanted me to be happy, of course. But, she also didn't because my getting married brought up her fear of losing me. It summoned those early childhood visions of her own mother being taken away from her by the man she would marry. And, again, those memories were hard to suppress.

Intellectually, she understood that people get married. Plus, she felt that if you're going to have children, then you should be married; that kind of went hand-in-hand. (My mother was very traditional that way.) Also, make no mistake—she thought very highly of Charles. She also respected the fact that his mother and father had been married for many years. And that he was very stable.

But all that didn't matter. When I got married, my mother was practically suicidal! You would have thought I'd just told her

I was moving to Australia and never coming back, and that she was never going to see me again. In her mind, she was losing me. Losing me to a man! Here she was giving me my dream wedding, and yet, as much as she may have thought she was keeping those feelings hidden, from the look on her face as we marched down that aisle, you would have thought she was walking the plank.

What you need to remember is that I worked for my mother as part of her team at Eartha Kitt Productions. We didn't live far from each other. I saw her almost daily. We spoke numerous times a day. The reality of our daily lives did not begin to justify the emotions that she expressed. But that was her feeling, which I came to understand better as I got older. I realized how much her childhood continued to impact her life into adulthood, and how hard it is to let go of those primitive experiences we have at a very young age.

When you have children of your own, you learn how hard it is to let those kids become themselves. Also, you can't imagine ever giving up your child!

When you have a child, you also know that you would do anything for him or her. Anything! Years later, after we had kids of our own, Charles would sometimes say to me that he would throw himself in front of a train for our children. And my response would be, "I would throw you in front of a train for our children, too." (Just kidding.)

But after my mother had a child of her own, she came to realize how incredibly painful it must have been for her own mother to have been willing to give her up and just walk away. Still, that was something that she was never able to truly forgive. How do you give in to a man who says, "I'm not going to let you have your child in your life?"

That stayed with her always, and I think that significantly impacted how she felt about men for the rest of her life. What happens to us in our early years is so formative. It establishes the narrative that we tell ourselves. And the narrative that my mother told herself was that she had been rejected and abandoned—for a man—and now it felt like I was doing it to her, too.

CHAPTER 28

The "Nana" Diaries

I have never yearned to stay young in the common sense,
but rather to stay me.

Charles and I soon moved to Westchester. We had been married for over three years when our first child, Jason, was born in 1990.

When my mother was pregnant with me, she gained all of about three ounces. By the time I had given birth to Jason, I was the size of a baby elephant. I worked out every day, and watched what I ate, but I just kept getting bigger and bigger. The doctor stopped weighing me after I gained sixty-seven pounds.

But here's an even weightier issue: Given the way my mother felt about me, you might expect that she would have been the world's best grandmother. Not quite! Most grandparents think their grandchildren can do no wrong. My mother was not that kind of grandparent. As much as she looked forward to seeing me experience motherhood, and was excited by the news that I was expecting, the reality of my children's existence was not what either of us had expected.

Don't get me wrong. She absolutely loved them. Adored them, even. But in many ways, my children took me away from her. They were rivals for my attention, not to mention a little too rambunctious for her taste at times.

To them, she was "Nana." The real question was, what should we name our kids?

I really wanted my son's name to be Justin. Until, that is, my mother said, "Oh, that'll be so cute! 'Just in case,' 'Just in time . . .'" To which I replied, "OK, we're not naming him Justin." We decided on Jason instead. But, funny enough, when my mother and I did a shoot for *People* magazine with Jason when he was six or seven months old, she told the magazine that his name was Justin, so that's what they wrote in the story. And for years afterward, she continued to say, "You really should have named him Justin. It's such a good name." I can see why my parents only had one name picked out for me. When my mother was set on something . . . that was it.

She also had a hard time, at first, with the fact that Jason was a boy. My mother had been so in love with me—this little girl that she doted on—that she couldn't quite understand how it was possible to give that same kind of love to a boy. Maybe, as the mother of a daughter, she just understood girls better. Or, given the negative impact that men had had on her life from the time she was a baby, maybe the truth was that she just fundamentally related better to girls.

This was very frustrating for me when Jason was young. I couldn't understand how she could not embrace him wholeheartedly, like I did. Not to mention that he looked so much like me, with blonde, curly hair, light eyes, and indecipherable features.

Another "walking United Nations."

My son may have been similarly hard to pinpoint racially, but there was one aspect of his identity that his father and I had agreed on before he was even born.

Charles and I had made the decision to raise our children in the Jewish faith. Neither of my parents had practiced any form of organized religion. My father had turned against Catholicism at an early age, and my mother, although not a believer in any particular practice, was extremely spiritual. She had always referred to "God," had read and learned a lot about many religions, and had taught me to have respect for ALL.

Because of that, I understood the importance religions and their traditions have for many people, and I felt it was necessary to give my children some sort of religious foundation, one that they could then choose to build on or not as they got older. I think I had always yearned to have that myself. And so, given that Charles and his family were practicing Jews, we decided that would be best for our children. (Decisions regarding religion are complex and fraught with controversy. I respect everyone's right to come to their own conclusions and make their own choices based on their personal beliefs. I hope, dear reader, that you feel the same.)

After my daughter Rachel was born, four and a half years later, my mother acknowledged that it had actually been good that I had given birth to a boy first. (As if I'd had any control over that.) "It's good you had a boy first," she said. "Now he can help take care of his little sister."

Other than that, my mother never really gave me much, if any, parenting advice. If she felt that my kids weren't being polite, she would just correct them directly. She wouldn't say to me, "You need to tell them to do X." She would tell them to do "X" herself.

This was far from a rare occurrence. Just as she had once insisted that I have perfect manners and grammar, she now expected the same things from them. If they said, "Hey, Nana, I want that," she would reply, "Excuse me? How do you ask for something properly?" She would step in and parent them directly. Remember the story about her encounter with the little prince?

Fortunately, my kids were pretty well-behaved. They were just often louder than my mother would have liked them to be, like most children are. OK, a lot louder! But, remember, she was used to having only one child. One little girl who was self-sufficient and played quietly by herself in the corner. The commotion of multiple children—one of whom was a boy, boys being oftentimes loud and boisterous—was more than her eardrums could sometimes tolerate.

She also couldn't understand that having two children doesn't make things twice as loud; it makes them ten times louder. Similarly, having a second child doesn't merely double your workload. The difference is exponential!

She didn't ever tell them to pipe down, though. She would just remove herself. This didn't necessarily mean that she left the house. She might just go sit in another room. Family dinners could often be sensory overload for her.

But she was very much part of the family. The fact that I never lived more than thirty minutes from her is amazing. She thought many times about buying an even larger property and creating a compound. "I'll buy this house for you guys," she would say, "and then there will be another house on the property for me."

Looking back on it, maybe I should have taken her up on that! But I think I knew that would have been a little too much togetherness, even though she was not an intrusive person. It's not as if she would just pop over all the time, because that wasn't her style. She liked to be by herself, in her own space, with her dogs.

It was knowing that I was accessible if she needed me that she liked. And, basically, I was. Accessible at all times. Wherever I moved, she ended up moving nearby. When Allan and I bought our current house in Connecticut, my mother soon purchased a house three miles up the road.

She didn't buy one down the block or right next door, though. She didn't want to be quite *that* close. As I said, there can be too much togetherness.

Consider the time that Rachel, my mother, and I did a photo shoot for *People* magazine in 1999. Rachel was only about four then, and Jason was almost ten. The article was about the three generations of women, though, so only Rachel was included with us in the photos. The problem was that she absolutely refused to cooperate during the shoot. She decided, as only a four-year-old can, that she was just not going to participate. She wouldn't smile and refused to listen to what anybody said.

I was desperate to get her to behave, so I recruited Jason to help with his little sister. "I need your help," I said to him. "Your sister is really giving me a hard time." He sat underneath the photographer's camera telling Rachel bathroom jokes.

Rachel absolutely idolized her brother, and she thought this was the funniest thing ever. Soon she was hysterical. She smiled, and the pictures came out amazing!

But my mother wasn't exactly pleased with either one of them. Not at all. Between Rachel's unwillingness to cooperate, and Jason's "off-color" humor, it was more than she could tolerate. Her discomfort with the situation was palpable, and I was now caught in the middle, wrangling a toddler, a nine-year-old boy, and a grown woman.

"Mom, she's cooperating, OK?" I said. "I know this isn't the kind of humor you like, and that you think it's disrespectful for a young boy to behave this way, and maybe you're not liking your grandson right now, but he *is* helping. So, please, let it go."

There were a lot of fun times with her, too, of course. Rachel and Jason both loved sitting on my mother's dressing room floor, having Chinese food picnics when she starred in the musical *The Wild Party* on Broadway in the year 2000. She would be onstage, then she would come back and sit down next to them and start eating out of the take-out cartons on the rug.

I think it's interesting, though, that my mother was never as motherly to my kids as she was to me, even in a grandmotherly way. As much as she loved them, she never really doted on them. And yet, if you looked in her bag, she had this huge photo album that she traveled with, filled with tons of pictures of them.

There were also many times when they got to come along with us when my mother was on the road. When she worked for Disney for many years—playing the role of Yzma in the animated movie *The Emperor's New Groove,* followed by the television series *The Emperor's New School*—they often flew out with us to California. They got to sit in the recording studio and watch the team of Disney animators sketch their grandmother while she voiced the words. Voice actors are filmed while they record, so when they put the sketched version of Yzma into motion, my kids got to see the evolution of the character from paper to moving image. How cool is that?

We worked on *The Emperor's New Groove* for four years. (Animated features take a long time.) One exciting part of that project for me was that Sting did the music for the film. I remember sitting in his New York apartment one day. My mother was at the piano standing next to Sting, and his musical director was playing as they rehearsed Yzma's song, "Snuff Out the Light." My mother and Sting were singing together, and I was looking out the window thinking, "OK, I'm good. They can take me now."

Another very cool experience was when my kids got to travel with us to Morocco when my mother performed for the king. There were a lot of perks that came with being my mother's grandchildren.

But not everything involving my mother and my kids was fun, or even acceptable. One of the biggest fights I ever had with her was over Jason, when he was a little boy.

It was during the holidays, on New Year's Day. My mother had performed at the Café Carlyle on New Year's Eve, and we were still at the hotel—my mother, Charles, Jason, Rachel, and me. I don't remember exactly what happened, but whatever it was had to do with the TV.

Jason must have done something—something that she didn't like. Maybe he changed the channel without asking her permission. Whatever it was, it upset her so much that she suddenly got up in a huff and walked out of the room.

He knew that he had done something to upset her, but he didn't know what. He was only a little boy. He looked at me with that little face, a face full of bewildered shock. A face that said, without his needing to utter a word, "Why did she walk away from me?"

So I followed my mother into the other room. I was furious at her. "You can't do that to a little boy!" I yelled. It wasn't right to make a child feel bad without explaining what he had done to upset her. "You have the obligation as an adult to tell him what it is." The "mother lion" in me was enraged.

My mother had known the pain as a small child of having adults be harsh, callous, or cruel to her. She should have known better than to behave that way herself.

I rarely yelled at my mother. But I was incredibly protective of my little boy. Unknowingly or not, my mother had crossed a line, and I had to stand up for him.

A part of her, I think, was shocked and taken aback that I was choosing sides, and I was choosing *his!* But another part of her understood that, as a mother, I had to protect my cub.

I don't remember if she went back and spoke to him that night. But it did change how she treated Jason from that day forward. I had shown her what was acceptable and what was not when it came to my children. There weren't any blurred lines there.

That was a significant turning point. A turning point for her, and for me as well.

Even as a teenager, I had never actually stood up to her. I'd never really rebelled. I'd never done anything to upset my mother, at least anything all that egregious. But my little boy took one look at me, and had my mother been a stranger, I would have jumped on her and tackled her to the ground.

I don't think she intentionally meant to hurt him. She was just doing her usual passive-aggressive thing, which, again, related to her abandonment issues. This sort of behavior had become her modus operandi. She didn't ever wait around to be abandoned. If someone did anything to hurt or offend her, she would leave first.

But I got that. I understood that she wasn't going to be the typical kind of grandparent—the doting kind. She had already given everything that she had to give. She had given it all to me.

She did love them, and they knew it. She may not have been the usual doting type, but she was very proud of them both. I would hear her talking to her friends about them. "My grandson is a star hockey player," she would boast. My mother knew zero about hockey. But she was still very proud.

That is not to say that she ever chose to watch Jason play in any of his games. If family dinners were too raucous and loud for her, how do you think a hockey game would have been?

You can only imagine what it was like for her to come to their birthday parties.

Rachel's birthday falls in July. We would always end up having a pool party for her just before the end of the school year. And not just a little pool party. A big one. I'd always say, "Rachel, you don't have to invite everybody. You don't need to ask the kids you only know to say hello to in the hall at school." But she wanted to invite everyone. She was that kind of kid.

My mother would come, too, and she would watch forty or fifty children screaming in the pool. (Not watch them all alone, of course. Lifeguards were always in attendance.)

"How do you tolerate all of this noise and craziness?" she would ask me.

All the commotion was a lot for her, but she would stay anyway. Probably because she knew that I wanted her to. There were a couple of kids who really loved my mother. They had seen her in *The Emperor's New Groove,* or the movie *Holes,* or perhaps their parents had told them she was famous, and they would come over to talk to her. They knew she wasn't the warm, fuzzy type, but she would often talk to them and ask them questions, and I think they were intrigued by her. Many of these kids knew her from her animated roles, and it's probably kind of cool to be in the presence of someone you know as a cartoon. Her natural edginess only made her more mysterious, I think.

We would always serve Twinkies at these parties in lieu of a birthday cake, because they were Rachel's favorite thing. And I remember there was this one little girl who was standing near my mother eating a Twinkie. Then she took another one, ate half of it, and spit the rest out.

"I don't want this," she said.

And my mother looked back at her with that famous look of hers, and said, "Really! And at just what point did you realize that?"

That was my mother for you. A woman who had an opinion about everything. Even a finger-shaped sponge cake.

CHAPTER 29

The New Brady Bunch

*Sometimes it's good to fall down to
see who will pick you up.*

After eleven years of marriage, Charles and I divorced. But then, about four years later, I got married again.

Allan Rothschild and I were introduced at a summer party by mutual friends who thought we would make a good match. We talked for hours that night, and the next night Allan asked me if I would accompany him to a friend's annual barbecue. While walking in the garden that second night, we found ourselves already discussing marriage. I was thirty-nine, and he was forty. We were both old enough to know what we were looking for.

We also knew right away that it was right. This relationship would work.

Allan was working as an executive at a real estate investment firm, but he was also a lawyer who had been raised on Long Island. He was also a divorced parent who, like me, shared joint custody of his own two children—a son, Eric, who was the same age as Jason, and a daughter, Nicole, who was two years older than Rachel.

I guess you could say that we were the new Brady Bunch. In fact, early in our marriage, Allan and I actually toyed with the idea of pitching our real-life version of the show as a television series, even if "The Rothschild Bunch" might not have had quite the same ring to it.

But I decided to keep my first married name, Shapiro, because it was the one that I shared with my children. Our lives were already complicated enough.

I think second marriages are a lot harder than first marriages, especially when there are children involved. You have a lot of people to deal with. A lot of personalities. And there's no training. Step-parenting makes parenting look easy.

Allan and I got married in May of 2002. When people ask me how long I have been married, I say thirty years. I figure that, between my two marriages, I've done the time. Besides, in many ways, we really are like one big, unique family. Charles and his wife, Cari, came to my wedding when I married Allan. So did Charles's parents, Judy and Ted. They sat next to Allan's parents, Rita and Stanley.

We're very lucky that everybody gets along so well.

When I agreed to move to the town where Allan lived in Connecticut, I asked Charles if he would consider moving there as well, to make it easier for him and Jason and Rachel to see each other. He said yes (a blessing that I am still grateful for), and bought a house not far from ours. Allan's ex-wife was already living there too, as well as one of his sisters and her family.

Then my mother bought a home nearby so that she could be closer to us as well. We all lived within a few miles of each other. It was truly a great set-up for the kids.

For all of us, actually.

But now the kids are all grown and living on their own and doing their own things. Eric, now thirty, is a teaching pro at a tennis facility. Jason, who is also thirty, used his athletic background to become an entrepreneur involved in sports marketing. Nicole, who is twenty-eight, worked at an investment bank and an impact investment fund (which involves making investments in underserved communities).

And then there's Rachel. At twenty-five, she is following in her grandmother's footsteps. After graduating from college, she became a professional singer/songwriter herself. (She uses the stage name Rachel Shaps.) Yes, the musical talent skipped a generation in our family, and I have gone from being "the daughter of . . ." to being "the mother of . . . ," but I'm good with that.

Whether or not you believe that "it takes a village," I know that it is certainly true for us. Those other things they say—"There's no 'I' in team," and "We're all in this together"—also apply to my family. In 2017, we all went to see Rachel graduate from Michigan

State University. And when I say "we," I mean Allan, me, Jason, Rachel, Eric, Nicole, and my ex-husband Charles, who still lives nearby, as well as his wife Cari and their twins, who are now fifteen. We were all in attendance for the entire weekend of festivities.

It was the ten of us. And my parents couldn't even be in the same room with each other for the four hours of my wedding! We really are a modern version of the Brady Bunch.

CHAPTER 30

Purrfectly Happy on her Own

The price we pay for being true to ourselves is worth it.

When my parents separated, in July of 1963, my mother had just turned thirty-six, and she was only thirty-seven when they divorced a year later. She was still young, and you would expect that she would have been eager to marry again. Or at least start dating again. But no.

Despite the kittenish quality that she projected onstage, she was more of a lion. Or lioness. Queen of the Jungle, and a self-sufficient creature if there ever was one. "Why would I want a man in my life?" she would ask whenever the subject came up.

"I have my child, and I have my career. Why would I need a man to make me feel whole?"

In that respect, she set an example for all women. She may not have made a name for herself as a feminist, specifically, but as a strong, independent woman she certainly lived as one in her everyday life, and she set an example for all independent-minded women for generations to come.

She had very conflicted feelings about men, though. From her own mother having abandoned her to marry a man who wouldn't accept her, to her own romantic experiences, I think she was reluctant to let a man into her life ever again.

I don't think that she trusted men on any level. She didn't trust them financially. And she certainly didn't trust them emotionally. My mother learned early on that the only person she could truly rely on was herself.

She was strong-willed and very set in her ways. She didn't understand that you can only make a relationship work through give and take. She felt that if a man was going to come into her life, then he was going to have to be the one willing to bend. She was never going to be the one to change or compromise.

My mother stated publicly many times that she didn't believe in compromise. There's a clip on YouTube in which she talks about it. The video has been referenced by many celebrities over the years, including Beyoncé, Jay Z, Miley Cyrus, and Jennifer Aniston. This video has been sampled many times because people find her statements about being independent so impactful. It's from a 1982 Christian Blackwood documentary called *All by*

Myself: The Eartha Kitt Story. In it, my mother is shown sitting outside in a garden, sipping tea while being interviewed as she talks about a woman's need to compromise in a relationship with a man.

"Can anyone live with Eartha Kitt?" the filmmaker asks her.

"That's not for me to decide," she replies, glaring at him, or perhaps the camera. "That's for someone who decides to live with me to decide, not for me."

"But are you willing to compromise within a relationship?" he persists.

"Compromise?" she asks disdainfully. "What is compromising? Compromising for what? Compromising for what reason? To compromise? For what? . . . What is 'compromise'?"

The answer is obvious, but the filmmaker does not give up pursuing the subject. "If a man came into your life, wouldn't you *want* to compromise?" he asks.

At this, she throws back her head and laughs uproariously. "Stupid! A man comes into my life, and *I* have to *compromise?* You must think about that one again." Then she throws back her head once more, laughs even more derisively, and demands, "A man comes into my life, and *I have to compromise?* For what? For what? For *what?*"

Personally, I have never understood that statement. How she could believe that. Or say those words.

I've always thought that compromise doesn't need to mean that you lose yourself. You have to be willing to compromise in order to have relationships with other people.

Whenever the subject would come up with my mother, it would always infuriate me. "That's just not right!" I would tell her. "You *have* to compromise! You can't live in society and not compromise."

Sure, I understand what she was saying. You don't compromise *yourself*. You don't compromise your values. You never compromise your principles or your beliefs. But you have to be able to give and take. You need to do that in any relationship.

My mother was always able to do that with me. Well, almost always. But she wouldn't do it with most other people, and she certainly wouldn't do it for a man. Her need for self-protection was intense. And that was part of her armor. She had been hurt too many times. And she wasn't going to change who she was for anybody.

So, if you were a man, and you were coming into her world, then you had better be strong, or at least flexible, because her expectations were very, very high.

And in her generation, few men were inclined to let a woman call the shots or "wear the pants." But my mother sure wasn't going to turn over the reins to anyone else. That is not to say that there weren't men who were pursuing her. Of course there were. But there was really nobody she dated for any length of time after my parents divorced. And she didn't ever complain about that.

The typical woman in her twenties, thirties, forties, and well beyond might joke about it. "Oh, I wish I could meet a man!" Not my mother, though. She said exactly the opposite. It was, "Why would I want a man in my life?" That was her fundamental attitude. She already had everything she wanted. Her career, her sense of self, and me.

I remember hearing her messages: "Never be dependent on a man." "Men are not to be trusted." Not to mention the ever-reliable, "Men are only interested in 'one thing.'" All coming from a woman who would stand up on a stage portraying the quintessential "sex kitten" and "material girl" (long before Madonna came along, she liked to point out).

So, how does a young girl differentiate this disapproving, overly suspicious, and fearful voice from the very public persona who shamelessly oozed sex on stage? And how did I end up so normal? (OK, loaded question. Definitely up for debate.)

As little girls, we tend to idolize our mothers, wanting to copy everything they do. And I was no exception. I would watch my mother perform over and over again, beaming with pride at the way the audience clung to her every facial expression and physical gesture. Her voice was described as sultry, feline, mysterious, and slightly dangerous. Her dancer's body was lithe, and her movements deliberate. But away from the spotlight, my mother was quite different from the slinky, beaded-gowned temptress who would captivate an audience with her unwavering stare. The woman I knew was quiet, reserved, powerfully calm, and extremely protective, not only of me, but also of her own internal pain. She had been disappointed and betrayed by so many.

Unfortunately, the guarded shield that she kept up helped keep her isolated from potentially meaningful relationships with anyone, aside from yours truly. The two things my mother feared most in life were being hurt in love, and losing me. Two messages that I received loud and clear. Two messages that carried a lot of weight. And, in the case of the second one, a lot of responsibility.

So I remember beginning to think, in my late teens and early twenties, "She's supposed to have somebody else! There's supposed to be another person in the picture. Not just me!" I didn't want to be what was essentially her one and only anymore. And there were times when I felt guilty about that.

But even earlier, as a little kid, I had begun to think, "Wait a minute. This isn't fair! I don't have any buffer, on any level. I have no other parent to buffer me, and I have no sibling to be a buffer." I sometimes felt the downside to being an only child of a single parent. I don't think I'm being egotistical when I say that, on some level, even as a little girl, I felt that families are not supposed to be just one person, or even two. There were important lessons to be learned that you could only learn from interacting with other humans. Humans other than your own parent. Lessons that you learned by fighting it out with others and getting your way, or maybe *not* getting your way.

When I was ready to have my children, I knew that I didn't want to have an only child. On the one hand, I loved being an only child because I got all of the attention. On the other hand, I didn't love being an only child *because I got all of the attention!*

When I became a mother, I knew that I wanted my children to have siblings, so that they could learn to share and coexist with others. And compromise!

My kids were born four and a half years apart, and when I saw them arguing over something when they were little, I would say to Jason, "Rachel is just a baby! You've got to give that to your little sister." And I remember thinking, "That's what you learn from siblings! These are the lessons you learn when you're not an only child."

I know a lot of people who love their siblings, and a lot of people who struggle to get along with them. But whether you love them or hate them, one thing you learn either way is that the world doesn't revolve around you. Sometimes you have to go to your brother's dentist appointment. Sometimes you have to give your sister the toy, even if it's only because Mom said so. Right? It's not because you want to, but because you have no choice. There are ways to interact with a sibling, or to treat someone, that supersede your immediate "want." Then, hopefully, you eventually learn to do those things voluntarily. There's so much that having a sibling teaches you in preparation for dealing with life.

You also learn that even when you have a conflict with your sibling, you're going to come home and he or she is going to still be there, whether you want them there or not. Mom isn't going to just move them out. That's a great way to learn to coexist with other people in this world. As an only child of a single parent, arguing and disagreeing sometimes comes at a great cost. Learning to fight can be filled with a complex web of emotions. Guilt is high up on that list.

So I knew early on that I didn't want only one child. My mother felt differently. She was fine having only one child and giving all of her attention to me.

She was also fine living on her own. I think she actually preferred it that way, which is probably why she readily agreed to get me my own apartment in the same building. Even after I was married, we never did live far from one another. But my mother always struggled with her fear that I was going to abandon her for my husband.

Abandonment remained her biggest fear. She always referred to it as "being rejected." Her choice of words alone reveals so much.

The reality, though, was that her fears, certainly with regard to me, were unfounded. Before Jason was born, I left a job I had taken in the fashion industry and went to work for my mother, as part of her management team, intertwining our lives even more. I always felt, deep down, that my mother needed me more than I needed her. And even through the times I yearned to be separate from her, I believed that it was necessary for me to be willing to step into those shoes. After all, I always felt that God had chosen *me* for *her.*

I continued to travel with her after I was married and my children were born, and, adding my business role to the mix, whenever she went to events that required a date—like the Emmys, the Grammys, or the Tony Awards—I was the one to usually go along as her "plus one."

My mother didn't really love attending industry events, though, because she wasn't someone who enjoyed getting all dolled up and going out on the town. Getting dressed up was what she did for work. Also, she didn't have the patience to listen to idle chitchat. My mother liked the art of conversation. She liked to sit with people whom she found interesting and have serious discussions about world events and social issues. But to go out and do the "schmoozing" thing? That was not easy for her. Similarly, it was sometimes even difficult for her to have patience in my house and listen to all of us chatter. My mother didn't care to hear about silly stuff, and gossip that was happening at school or with other children that my kids knew. She would literally tune that out. She had nothing to say about it and no interest in hearing it.

If you sat down next to her and started talking about current events or politics, though, or something that she viewed as socially important or meaningful to the world, then you had her full attention. But she wasn't that interested in talking about fashion, or the latest beauty product or other trivialities. To her, that was a total waste of energy.

The thing is, that's what people generally talk about when they go out together. And families often sit around discussing the mundane, personal events of their days. It's not because they're being frivolous. That's just what people do—they make small talk. Most people don't sit around having philosophical discussions every time they encounter another person. I think that would be exhausting! When adults go out to dinner, they tend to talk about their kids and mutual interests, or ask, "Seen any good movies lately?"

But the trivial details of other people's lives were not what interested my mother. She wanted to engage in more serious discussions. That's what she would say: "I want to be intellectually stimulated by other people."

When she had first started out in Paris, and she was hanging out with Orson Welles and his friends, they would sit around in cafés for hours, discussing books, literature, art, and other engaging topics. She found it fascinating! She said that she often didn't speak a word the entire night. She would just sit there listening, absorbing what all of these sophisticated people had to say. Having never even finished high school, my mother took this to be a learning experience, and so she soaked up the diverse knowledge of Welles and his cronies. To her, huddling among these interesting people, as they engaged in heated debates and flaunted their incredible intellects, was equivalent to sitting in on the highest-level college classes. Those evenings motivated her to learn more about the many esoteric subjects to which she was being exposed. The next day, she would often be found in the library, filling that void.

That's largely how she educated herself. Watching and listening. Soaking up the situations in which she found herself. She enjoyed being with people who might stimulate her intellectually and broaden her knowledge. That made her feel alive! But she was not particularly interested in companionship for its own sake, or in going out on a date just because it was what other people thought she should do.

And I wasn't that interested in her dating either. I was extremely possessive of my mother, which I can only imagine would have been quite the obstacle for any would-be suitor. I remember one man who my mother briefly dated. The first time I met him, he was taking her out to dinner. I also remember that I instantly didn't like him. It's possible that this wasn't personal, and I just objected to the idea of any man taking her out to dinner. I was only about ten at the time. I remember throwing a bottle of ink on his light-colored suit that night. This wasn't received well. By either of them.

Remember, though, that my mother had raised a child she was incredibly attached to, and who was incredibly attached to her. It wasn't easy for anyone to come between us. My behavior might not have stopped the average person, but it was enough to stop my mother. Their relationship didn't last long.

Later on, my mother dated another man named Peter. He was very tall and very blonde. I don't remember him beyond that. But I didn't particularly like him, either.

I guess I wasn't much of a fan of compromise, either.

Ultimately, between her work schedule, working in her garden, her home, her animals, and me, I think my mother felt her life was fully nourished.

CHAPTER 31

Eartha's Earthly Possessions

I don't have to be wealthy to be rich.

My mother may have played the part of the original "Material Girl" onstage, but that was not the real her. In real life, she was never one to want a lot of material things. What was important to her was the home that she lived in and the land that it was situated on. In that respect, she had nice things because she always had a beautiful home and plenty of land to go with it.

But she didn't really care about things themselves. Despite all the fancy gifts she had been given by many of her early suitors, she didn't own, or want, a lot of jewelry. "I'm a dirt person," she told

Ebony magazine in 1993. "I trust the dirt. I don't trust diamonds and gold."

Neither did she collect expensive art. Everything that she surrounded herself with had real significance to her—but significance because it had some sort of personal or sentimental value. Yes, many had monetary value, too. But to her, it was always more about her emotional connection with those items, rather than their actual economic worth.

The items that my mother treasured most of all were pieces she had obtained in her travels, and gifts given to her by fans. If a person had gone out of his or her way to give her something, whether a card or a present, then she would treasure it. It didn't matter if it was big or small, or whether it was purchased or handmade. These gifts had come from the heart. And because of that, she displayed them proudly in her house. My mother would say that her fans gave her emotional support. Because of them, she felt seen and heard. That acceptance meant the world to her.

She could tell you where many pieces she owned had come from—who had given them to her, in what theater, what country, and approximately what year. Those were the things with which she wanted to surround herself. When she came home, she would be in this safe haven, this womb, surrounded by love, because all of these treasures contained love.

Her home was her sanctuary. It was where she went to regroup and recharge. Being on stage and in the limelight, as energizing as that could be, was also physically and emotionally draining. As exciting as it was to travel the world, home was the destination that my mother always looked forward to most.

And so she chose those homes with care. She always made sure that they had enough land for her vegetable garden, as well as some body of water. Preferably running water. My mother loved the water! Her final home was on a river, from which she got much enjoyment during her final days. Her prior two homes had ponds, so she had them aerated to create the sound of movement.

Interestingly enough, her first home, the one in Beverly Hills, had no natural water at all. Only a swimming pool. So, did her need for water evolve over time? Or had she just ignored it early on? Ironically, since she believed for so many years that she had been born on January 26—under the astrological sign of Aquarius, a water sign—maybe she didn't feel the need to live near water as much as when she eventually discovered that she had actually been born on January 17, and she was a Capricorn, an earth sign. After all, earth cannot exist without water. As strong as my mother's connection with Nature was, this cannot be pure coincidence.

It seems funny to me now that she never bought a house on the beach. Although, as I think about it, it actually makes sense. My mother was rich and deep, like well-fertilized soil, not grainy and unsteady, like the sand. Not much grows in sand. And when she would return to her home, she would reconnect with Nature and that soil. Digging in her garden truly took her back to her roots and helped reinvigorate her soul.

As for the things she kept inside her home, her style was eclectic. . . . Combined with the gifts from her fans, you would find some of my childhood paintings, framed as if they were Picassos (definitely an only-child perk); lots of her needlepointed pieces (and I do mean LOTS); and countless items she had collected through the years, from furnishings and awards to photographs and ephemera.

Whatever it was, she kept it. Kept it all! You could say my mother was a bit of a hoarder.

As I went through her house after she died, I discovered hundreds of things I had never seen before. One was just a napkin. No writing. No design. Just a plain white napkin. I would look at it and wonder, "Why did she keep this particular napkin? Was it Marlon Brando's? Was it from someplace that I should know about? Do I throw it out? What was she keeping it for?" (I think I kept it, since I just wasn't sure.)

There were scripts from productions that she had performed in, as well as some of the gowns that she had worn throughout the years in her one-woman show. Some of these dresses had been made by well-known designers, such as Pierre Balmain, Isaac Mizrahi, Zac Posen, and Marc Bouwer. But often she went to costumers in the theater community because she moved around onstage a lot and wanted them designed specifically to have ease of movement.

Most of the clothing she kept was also of sentimental rather than necessarily monetary value. Then there are all the notes and notebooks. Along with being a voracious reader, my mother was an avid writer. She would keep a notepad and pen within reach at all times, jotting down thoughts and ideas both day and night. If she happened to hear something she liked, then she would write it down. Kind of ironic, because when it came to speaking, my mother was a woman of few words. She would choose her words carefully. And she often wished others would do the same. There were times when you would be explaining something to her, and if you repeated yourself, or elaborated too much, she would look at you and say, "Too many words!" She was impatient with inefficiency and excess. So if you were speaking to her, and you went on and on, provided that she knew you well enough, she would just stop you cold.

To her, you said it once, you said it efficiently, and you didn't have to say it again.

But when it came to writing, she, herself, had a lot to say. And I do mean a lot! She was very prolific. I now have mounds and mounds of paper, probably thousands of pages of handwritten notes. Some are in journals, dating back to the 1940s and '50s. A few are written in beautiful, leather-bound books. Like many of us, my mother would start a journal, write in it for the first twenty or thirty pages, and then suddenly there would be nothing. And what is written in them consists mostly of mundane musings.

"Today I had dinner, then went to rehearsal. Tomorrow I'm meeting so-and-so. The show went well." They're very similar to what almost anybody would write. But not always. There's one entry, for example, that says, "Frank is meeting us . . ." and she was, in fact, referring to Frank Sinatra. Occasionally, there will be little throw-away comments like that. But for the most part, her journal entries sound just like almost anyone else's.

It's interesting now to see the items my mother did keep—all the letters, contracts, scripts, and travel itineraries. I think she kept them because it was important for her to remember every step of her path through life; the difficult ones, as well as the ones that were joyous. Every one of them kept her real.

They also kept her grounded.

No matter what happened, she never became full of herself. Yes, she knew that she had talent. Knew that she was famous. Those are things that she definitely understood. As someone who had always respected her elders, as my mother aged, she felt that she deserved a certain level of respect based on both her age and the degree of success she had attained in life.

But she was never one who took anything for granted. All of her possessions served as reminders. Reminders of the past. They were there to help her remember. *This* was the road you traveled. *This* was how you got to where you are now.

She really believed in the idea that everything in life happens for a reason. So it's important to embrace all of those moments in life, and to dissect them in order to learn from them, appreciate them, and maybe not make the same mistakes again.

And similar to the way that she said I gave her roots—gave her the family that she had always yearned for—maybe having these items helped her to stay rooted. Grounded her even more deeply.

There are two letters, in particular, that my mother received in the 1960s that are good examples of this. Both, I assume, are reactions to a performance she had done on TV. One letter was clearly written by a white woman, and the other by someone who was Black. Both criticize her vehemently, but for entirely different reasons. In the first case, she was chastised for "acting like she's white," and in the other for "acting like she's Black." (Highlighting, once again, how she didn't really conform to either race.) I can only imagine how wounding those words must have been for her to read.

And yet she kept them anyway.

This sort of criticism didn't necessarily offend my mother, you see. Rather, she found such comments to be interesting statements about the human race; about hatred, anger, racism, and people's need to put others down just because they're not like them. She found these letters to be so significant that she kept them for all those decades. I'm not sure if she ever responded to them, although knowing her she probably did. On some level, she understood that there are certain people you don't dignify with a response. Yet she was often willing to engage people in meaningful discussions about difficult topics like these, regardless of their points of view.

My mother held onto all of these things because she felt that every single thing she owned—along with every emotion, inter-action, and experience she'd had—comprised the person that she evolved to be. Everything, positive or negative, contributed to the richness of who she was.

CHAPTER 32

On the Road Again

I search for truth while I prepare for the shock of it.

My mother never knew exactly what day, or even year, she had been born. She had always merely speculated about her age, as well as who her father had been. Then, in 1998, when she was seventy-one years old, she went to speak at Benedict College in Columbia, South Carolina, one of the HBCU (Historically Black Colleges and Universities). It is located near the town of North, South Carolina, where my mother had been born. I was with her that day.

"I've never been able to find a copy of my birth certificate," she told the students. "If somebody here could find a copy. . . ." She challenged them to locate one. They could have assumed that she was just joking, but a group of those students took her up on it. And guess what? They actually managed to track it down.

At least they found out that there was one, and where it was located. They weren't able to obtain it themselves, of course, because of state privacy laws. But upon learning this news, my mother hired a lawyer to petition the courts to allow us access to it. There had always been much speculation as to the identity of her father, and she was anxious for the opportunity to finally learn the truth. She assumed that his name would be on there.

After a few months of filing considerable amounts of paperwork, the court said that it would allow both my mother and me access to the birth certificate. We would only be permitted to view it inside a judge's chambers, however. We were told that we could not obtain a copy of it, nor would we be allowed to even take a picture of it. In fact, we would only be allowed fifteen minutes to view the document in the presence of the judge. Why, you may ask? I can honestly say that I don't even remember myself. It was all so crazy.

My mother and I flew down to the courthouse in Columbia, South Carolina, and nervously entered the judge's chambers. And guess what. The father's name had been redacted!

It was totally blacked out!

Incredibly, the only pertinent information that remained visible was my mother's name and date of birth, her mother's name, and the name of the midwife. Her father's name—the only thing we had really wanted to know—was completely unreadable.

The judge explained that this was not unusual for the time (the 1920s) when a child was born out of wedlock, as midwives were often instructed to hide the name of the father in order to protect him (and his family).

My mother was shaken. And speechless. All these years later, and her father's identity was still being kept hidden from her! It just didn't seem fair. We left the courthouse in shock.

We did find out one thing that was very interesting, though. It turned out that she had been born on January 17, 1927, not January 26, 1926, as she had always thought. She had been celebrating her birthday on the wrong day for seventy-one years! Not to mention that she was a year younger than she had believed herself to be. This also meant that she went from being an Aquarian—a Water sign—to a Capricorn, an Earth sign. How fitting is that?

No wonder her given name was Eartha! Seeing that she was an earth sign, her name suddenly made perfect sense.

My mother never did get to find out who her father was, though. I can only imagine how that must have felt. Our identities are so tied up with the information that we are given about who we are—the year and day that we were born, as well as the day of the week, who our parents are, the town that we're from, the state that we're from, the country we're from, the religion we believe in or don't believe in, and the traditions and customs of the society in which we live. There are so many ways that we identify ourselves: I am so-and-so; I was born on this day; in the town of this; and the country of that; and these are the names of my parents. I wonder what it does to a person, psychologically and emotionally, to never know some of these basic things. To never really know who you truly are.

CHAPTER 33

God Only Knows

I glorify in that which I cannot see; it makes me think.

At least I knew where *I* came from. Except when it came to religion, that is. In that respect, I wasn't really anything. Neither of my parents had believed in organized religion. My father had grown up in a very devout Catholic family. My grandmother had sent him to Catholic school, and he had very unpleasant memories of it. That experience turned him against organized religion.

My mother remembered singing in the Baptist church choir as a young girl in the South, but she hadn't had any formal religious schooling and had never believed in organized religion. She also felt that organized religion had been responsible for almost every war that has ever been waged. People had been fighting over religion since the beginning of time, she said, so she found it difficult to see it as a positive thing. Yet she was the most spiritual person I've ever met, and she definitely believed in a Higher Power of some kind. She would refer to that power as God because that's the name that works for most people.

My mother didn't go out of her way to introduce me to any form of religion. Quite the opposite. Even though she made sure that we visited many houses of worship when we traveled, that had been mainly to understand the beliefs of other cultures. She wanted me to understand them, too, but she was very clear that she did not want me raised worshipping any particular God.

The times that she traveled without me when I got older, though, she left me with Mrs. McCoy, our housekeeper, who was a Jehovah's Witness. Attending religious services was very important to Mrs. McCoy, so if I was in her care on those days, she would sometimes take me with her. Years later, my mother would tell stories about how she would come home from work and I would be preaching the Bible to her.

I'm not really sure how accurate a memory that was, nor do I think that I was actually "preaching." Maybe I would simply refer to something I had heard in a sermon. As I grew older, I began to wonder if what my mother had perceived as "preaching" was just my own desire or yearning to search for something bigger than myself or my mother's beliefs.

I believe that children yearn for rules and boundaries. They want something that will provide a sense of control over their lives, or at least some structure. So when I met my first husband, Charles, we began to talk about how we were going to raise our children. "What are they going to be?" we wondered. It was important, we agreed, for them to have a foundation.

As I mentioned, I hadn't been raised with any religion. The only reason my mother and I celebrated Christmas was because that's what most people do in this country. You get a Christmas tree in December, you buy presents, and you celebrate Christmas.

But my husband didn't celebrate Christmas. He was Jewish. He had been raised in the Jewish faith, and he wanted to raise our children in the Jewish faith as well. Having no conflicting beliefs, I thought that this made a lot of sense. Judaism is not just a religion. It has a long history of culture and traditions. These, I felt, were things that were really important for our children to have. Through my travels with my mother, I had learned to be respectful of and appreciate all people's traditions.

After the decision was made with regard to our unborn children, I was faced with the question of whether I should convert to Judaism myself. It was explained to me that I would need to study, then go before a rabbinical court, where the Rabbis would ask, among other things, "If it weren't for marrying Charles, would you be taking on this religion?" I couldn't lie.

I had too much respect for religion, and its importance to so many, to not be honest about it. And the reality was that I would not have chosen to take on that religion if I hadn't married Charles.

Charles, though, being a lawyer and very pragmatic, had an idea. "What if we converted the children after they were born?"

he asked the Rabbi. "Would they then be able to be raised in the Jewish faith?"

And the Rabbi said, "Yes!"

Our children had to officially convert because I wasn't Jewish myself, and Judaism, by tradition, is matrilineal, meaning that it is considered to be passed down through one's mother. So when Jason was four months old, we had to go to a mikvah—a special bath used in Judaism for ritual immersion as part of the conversion ceremony.

The mikvah that we went to was located in a townhouse in Brooklyn. It was so beautiful that it was almost like a spa. Charles put on a bathing suit, and Jason wore his birthday suit. Charles walked into the water carrying Jason, and the Rabbi said some prayers. When the prayers were finished, Charles had been instructed to blow in Jason's face, so that he would hold his breath, and then dunk him in the water, completing the process.

When Rachel was converted, a few years later, we went back to the same mikvah. Afterward, when we were driving home, Jason, who was four and a half years old, turned around and said, "Mommy, now you're the only one who's not on the Jewish team!"

When Jason and Rachel were little, they went to nursery school at the JCC—the Jewish Community Center. Later, they attended public school, but after school they both went to Hebrew school. I still remember taking Rachel to a children's service when she was four or five.

"Where are we going, Mommy?" she asked along the way.

I said we were going to a service for *Shabbat,* the Hebrew word for the Sabbath.

"Where is it?" she asked.

"In the temple," I replied.

"What's the temple?" she asked.

When children are little, you want to give them the simplest explanation possible. So I gave her the easiest answer I could think of. I said we were going to God's house.

Later, we were sitting in the temple during the service. The Rabbi and the Cantor were standing up at the Bima before everyone, when Rachel turned to me and whispered, "Mommy! Which one's God?"

Kids are so literal. What else was she going to think? After all, I had told her we were going to somebody's house. The person who owns the house should be there.

Later, Jason and Rachel had their bar mitzvah and bat mitzvah, respectively, the traditional coming-of-age ceremonies held when a Jewish child turns thirteen. In each case, I stood beside them and read the prayer designated for the mother. I read it in English. Then Charles read the prayer for the father in Hebrew.

I'm really glad that we gave our kids that foundation. I think that, whatever religion you practice, it teaches you the basics of how to treat others. Most religions believe that you should treat other people kindly, help the needy, and respect your parents and your elders. These are important fundamental teachings.

That is not to say that people who do it differently are doing it wrong. This is a very personal decision. We made what was the right choice for our family.

My mother didn't quite understand that, though. She didn't understand the need for my kids to be brought up with any religion. She felt that her own religion was Nature. Her spirituality was so rooted in Nature and the universe that I'm not sure you could legitimately say she wasn't religious just because she didn't go to church or synagogue. Her "House of Worship" just didn't have a roof. After all, she read religious books from all different walks of life. And she really gave me a strong ethical foundation, the kind that most people are taught through religion.

I think what she didn't care for was that I had imposed a specific category on my kids. My mother didn't like categories of any kind.

I have a picture of my mother when she was about six years old taken in the South, standing in front of the local Baptist church in her little choir gown. But I don't think she had much exposure to religion beyond that.

She certainly didn't experience the devout people in her hometown treating her with much kindness or care. So I'm not sure she believed that religion "worked" when it came to her. Most likely, she thought, "Here are these people who are supposedly God-fearing, yet they are beating a helpless child."

Still, my mother accepted and went along with the program after my kids were born. She would always come to our Passover seders, and to our High Holiday dinners on Rosh Hashanah and Yom Kippur, and she would also come over to celebrate Hanukkah. These traditions were not something that she would ever have done on her own, obviously, but she respected them and our decision to keep them.

Later, after I married Allan, she really enjoyed living so close by and would always be at our big holiday dinners with multiple generations of our blended family in attendance: Jason, Rachel, Allan, his children, Eric, and Nicole, Allan's parents, his cousins, and his sisters and their families. It really didn't make any difference to her whether these celebrations were for Passover or for Christmas. Everyone being together as a unit—that was what she had always yearned for. These were cherished times for my mother. She truly loved being a part of our big, crazy family.

CHAPTER 34

A Hard Act to Follow

You have to take a chance in order to enhance.

As I look back now, the one thing I wish my mother had done when I was a kid was push me to get a job. A weekend job. Summer job. After school . . . whenever. There is so much a person learns from having a job and needing to show up to work. If there's one thing my mother did not shy away from, it was hard work. No matter how tough things got, she was someone who always managed to cross the finish line. But I was not my mother. There have been many times when I've been willing to say, "I'm okay with not finishing."

Here's a simple example of that: When I'm doing a workout, my friend, Julie, who I train with, will often give me a goal. "You have to do a hundred sit-ups," she might say.

When I get tired, I'll respond, "Eh! I don't think I have to do a hundred. I'm perfectly okay with sixty-two."

And she'll say, "Who stops at sixty-two? At least do seventy or seventy-five. Nobody stops at sixty-two!"

Well, I do. At least there's a piece of me that does. I stop at sixty-two if I've had enough.

Definitely not my mother. She had mental grit. She could be utterly exhausted, yet she wouldn't ever give up.

I'm a different person. I don't have her level of determination. I think this frustrated my mother at times, even though she never really voiced it.

Maybe that was because she saw potential in me, in so many different areas. She thought that I could have been a great dancer. Or a great writer. Or photographer. "You have a great brain," she would also say. "You could be an unbelievable lawyer!" To her, everything that I did was great.

It's wonderful to have a parent who is that supportive. But it doesn't help you figure it all out. Instead, for me, it was, "So, you're telling me I can be a mounted policewoman-photographer-CEO-writer-model."

I'm not sure if she ever actually told me that I could be president when I grew up, but she probably said that, too. In her mind, I could have been anything I wanted to be. But as a child, I sometimes felt, "Well, that's not really helpful." As encouraging as all that validation may have been, it didn't help me focus on any one direction.

My mother thought I was great at everything. Yes, hearing that message from a parent is wonderfully empowering. But as a young girl, I sometimes wanted to yell, "Hello? Just tell me that I'm supposed to be *this*."

I had many interests, but I didn't have that strong a desire to do any one thing in particular. Especially since my mother said that I could do everything. And do it all fabulously.

A little girl, hearing that, might walk around feeling very proud. But then, as a teenager and young adult, she starts to think, "What exactly *do* I do?"

I had been told I could do everything. Well, that's not right. Or fair. I think it would have been more helpful if I'd been given some guidance on how to better channel all my interests.

But my mother didn't quite understand what it was like not to have inner drive. She was motivated from Day 1. She had no choice. For her, it was a matter of survival. Her mindset was, similarly, "Who stops at sixty-two? Who *does* that?" If asked to do 100 of something, my mother would have done 110. She always felt that she had to prove herself even more.

My mother was also someone who felt that you had to figure things out on your own. *She* sure had to. I, on the other hand, found that frustrating. "I don't want to figure it out on my own," I would reply. "What am I supposed to do? Tell me which path to take!"

"I can't tell you what to do," she would say. "You have to come to that decision yourself."

So I dabbled in lots of things. I loved photography. I loved interior design. I loved writing. But I never believed that I was actually creative enough for any of those fields. I'll go one step further. I never actually thought of myself as being creative at all. Strange, considering that everything I was interested in involved creativity.

So, as much as I sometimes thought, "Well, maybe I'll go into modeling," or "Maybe I'll go into acting," and I dabbled with various other possibilities here and there, I never pursued any one of them with real passion. I never tried to make a name for myself, either. Maybe that was because I never yearned to be the one with the name. I was always OK with my mother being the famous person.

I do think that, on some level, I tried to avoid the spotlight out of a fear of competition. I'm not sure if I was more afraid of failure or success. You know, what would happen if I did become the more famous one? What would happen if I did become successful? Where does that put my mother? How does that change the dynamic between us?

These are only questions that I've asked myself. I've wondered. But I don't really know the answers.

I think, to a certain extent, I didn't go into the entertainment business because it felt like those shoes were already filled. It's not like I was going to be Liza Minnelli to Judy Garland. But I wasn't looking at other options either. I think I saw it as, "You either follow in your mother's footsteps, and you become a performer, or you pursue something that has nothing whatsoever to do with being onstage."

But I had grown up as a natural entertainer. I loved to entertain my grandmother, my aunts, and other family members, but most of all I loved performing for my mother—to sing and dance for her. As a little girl, I would always make up dances. She would often perform at Caesars Palace in Las Vegas, and one of the times that she was there, Juliet Prowse was performing in the musical *Sweet Charity*. She was in the same theater there while my mother was in whatever headliner room that she was in. I loved musicals. Loved them! So I would go watch *Sweet Charity* every night.

My mother loved to tell the story of how, one night, when she was in her dressing room, I said, "Mommy, you sit there and turn off all the lights. I'm going to perform a song for you." Then I went into the bathroom and got this big mink stole that my mother used in her act. It was like a long scarf—one piece of mink after another. I was only about six or seven at the time. I got this big, furry thing and wrapped it around and around myself, and then I came out of the bathroom in it. She thought I was going to perform one of the many sweet songs from *Sweet Charity*. Instead, I came out and began singing "Hey, Big Spender."

"The minute you walked in the joint—boom! Boom!—I could see you were a man of distinction, a real big spender! Hey, big spender, spend a little time with me!"

I had no idea what I was doing, of course. It was just my favorite song in the show, and I was copying how I had seen Juliet Prowse perform it onstage. But my mother almost fell off her chair laughing.

Then there was the comedy routine for which Red Skelton was famous, in which he played a drunk swigging Gordon's Dry Gin. I learned this entire routine, too. How funny was it to see an eight- or nine-year-old girl playing a drunken old man? I did it so spot-on, my mother said, that she would often have me perform it for people that she knew. They would sit down in the living room, and I would do my Red Skelton skit. Everyone thought it was a riot!

I think I loved performing mostly because I loved making my mother smile, though. I loved to make her laugh. Plus, I was a child of the entertainment business, right? What else was I going to do? I wasn't going to sit there and do math problems.

I had developed a very vivid imagination in the hills of our Beverly Hills home with my two dogs. So I would play around and make up dance routines and all sorts of other things. And my mother would just beam with pride.

My mother always told me I was the funniest person who had ever lived, and I believed her. It's hard to get that sort of response out of your husband, of course—or your children, for that matter. Once, when Jason was a teenager, he asked me why I had walked into his room, and I told him, "I'm here to collect the rent." He just rolled his eyes and said, "Mom, you are so not funny." My husband does the same thing. I'll say something and totally crack myself up, and he'll say, "I don't get it. What was so funny about that?"

"Well, my mother would think it was funny," I'll reply. She thought everything I said was funny. Granted, perhaps she wasn't the most objective critic. Maybe my antics wouldn't ever have translated into my having a professional career as a stand-up comic.

When I was a teenager, I really wanted to be a dancer. I had always loved ballet. But that would have required working excruciatingly hard, and I wasn't willing to give up having a life for dance. I wasn't willing to give up having a life to be *anything*.

Still, whatever I did, my mother thought I was amazing at it. And then when I didn't pursue it, she would say, "I don't know why you didn't follow through with that!"

I look back now and wonder, did I step away from show business intentionally? What was I avoiding? Was it the fear of success? Or fear of failure? I don't know which it was. Probably both. I think both can be equally frightening at times.

Then there was another issue. So many people wish that they could be famous. But I knew what fame was like already. I knew the upside, and also the downside. I knew that fame wasn't all that everyone imagines it to be.

I had learned that when you're famous, you don't always have the freedom to just *be*. You can't go out and just act carefree. That probably hasn't changed much. Maybe it's even gotten worse. Celebrities these days really can't go anywhere. I can't imagine what it would have been like for my mother if there had been cellphones back then.

It's not that I wish she hadn't encouraged and lavished so much praise on me. I know she was coming from a well-meaning place, wanting to give your child confidence and the ability to soar—a feeling that she, as a young girl, had never had herself.

But the result was that I didn't ever choose to go off on my own path. I always remained attached to my mother. I never lived more than a few miles away from her and saw her almost daily throughout my entire life. Which is ironic, given that I grew up with the woman whose main motto, more or less, was, "Never be dependent on anyone."

But I felt that she somehow needed me more than I needed her. Emotionally, for sure. I wasn't ever going to go very far away from her, anyway. And I sure wasn't going to pursue any career that was going to take me away from her.

That's how I finally ended up with the one job that worked for us both: being my mother's manager. And *that* was a career—one that brought us together even more.

CHAPTER 35

My Mother's Keeper

I stayed on my path and did not follow the herd.
I made a way for myself.

I was shy when I was a little girl. So shy that I hid behind my mother's skirts. But then, as I got older, I became the more gregarious one of the two of us. No, I didn't ever stand on a stage, but it was almost as if, in certain situations, she was the one hiding behind *my* skirt.

People might have assumed that she was acting aloof at first because she was a celebrity. What they didn't know was that my mother was extremely shy. They may have just figured that she was a diva who didn't care to speak. But that wasn't it at all. She would have been the first to attribute it to her shyness. When I was younger, I would sometimes say to her, "Stop! Please show everyone that you're actually a very nice person. Don't let them think that you're not. Show them that you're warm and fuzzy!"

When she would walk into a room in which there were strangers, whether it was for a photo shoot, personal appearance, or interview, she would often be the one standing behind me. I would be the one to take the lead and say, "Hi, we're here," and then introduce myself. "I'm Kitt, Eartha's daughter. Where should we go?" I was often the one who would have to "break the ice," never being sure how long it would take my mother to feel at ease enough to let down that protective wall and relax.

I could always feel her tense up as strangers would approach, greeting us, making conversation, and inquiring as to our needs. It would take a few minutes for her to let down her guard, or even longer at times. But then, as she sat in the makeup chair with Carlo by her side, or Milagros (another makeup artist who was a member of our team for many years), she would begin the transformation from Eartha Mae to Eartha Kitt. Her defensive barrier would start to dissipate and her natural charm would be revealed. Then someone would bring her coffee, and as people began to make chitchat around us, she would become more comfortable. I would be talking to one person or another, her makeup would start to be applied, and she would begin to warm up.

After a while, she wouldn't want to leave, and people who had been walking on eggshells around her at first wouldn't want her to leave, either, because they had realized, "Oh, my God, this woman is so real and so down to earth and so wonderful!"

But if you had left before that evolution had taken place, then you might have found my mother quite intimidating. The Eartha Kitt persona is what they saw, even though she began with no makeup on. She would enter a room with that kind of control, a defense mechanism that she used as self-protection. She carried herself that way. People would be whispering, "That's Eartha Kitt! What do we do? What do we say?" They would be cowering because they were fearful. I'm not sure what they were afraid of. But if they stuck around and saw that she was a real person, with some trepidation of her own, then they would come to realize, "Wow! What was I so nervous about? She's the coolest lady ever!"

Still, sometimes I would walk into a room behind her and whisper, "Be nice!" Because I knew her shyness could come across as diva-esque.

Being up on a stage, standing taller than the crowd, creates a sort of barricade. Onstage, you really are in command. You're the one up there, and everyone else is down in their seats. The audience in attendance has paid to come see you, and you're the one in control.

When you walk into a room where everyone is standing on the same level, though—especially if you don't know them, and you are as tiny as my mother was—it's easy to feel vulnerable. My mother sure did. That alone could make her feel defenseless, which took her right back to the South, where she had been even tinier. She had been just a little peanut.

I understood the root cause of what others may have perceived as her being stand-offish, or sometimes acting like a "diva." She also understood that about herself, and would sometimes worry, saying, "Some people probably thought I was not so nice. They didn't know I was shy."

This was far easier to overcome when she was in full makeup. Makeup serves as a mask in many ways. In full attire, walking into a room dressed in a gown or costume, with hair and makeup done, my mother was not nearly as vulnerable as when she was just Eartha Mae. Eartha Mae had been completely unprotected in the South. They had beaten the crap out of her.

Over the years, I had gotten used to managing situations for my mother in this way. So after a while, it only made sense that I should become her official manager. She felt most comfortable having me serve as her front man because she knew I would always have her back.

My mother was the consummate artist. Onstage, she didn't just know what to do and how to do it. She excelled at it. She didn't want to have to also worry about all the nitty-gritty details on the business side of her performances and touring. So I handled a lot of that. Beginning in around 1991, I started working for her and traveling with her, when necessary. I joined her team, which included her longtime musical director, Daryl Waters; a core group of musicians; her personal assistant, Jaki; and either Carlo or Milagros doing hair and makeup.

I assisted with all logistical aspects of the performances, including but not limited to travel arrangements for the entourage, hotel and dressing room needs, supplemental musicians, and coordinating press interviews and photo sessions. I also served as the direct connection to her. That allowed her to focus completely on the most important piece, the performance itself.

Given my personality, there was another benefit. When my mother wasn't singing, she was very conscientious about keeping quiet. Speaking can be quite taxing on the vocal cords and can take a lot more out of you than singing. So the less a singer can talk before a performance, the better. That's another reason she liked to have me around. I could talk enough for both of us. Hey, I was an only child. At times, mine was the only voice I heard. I was perfectly capable of holding both sides of a conversation. As comfortable as I have always been with "peace and quiet," I am quite good at filling in the silences as well. Oftentimes, I served as my mother's vocal cords off the stage.

During the many years that I was her manager, we got around. The world, I mean. My mother performed in almost every major city, and some not so major, not only in the U.S., but Europe, Africa, Canada, Scandinavia, Australia, and Asia as well.

We also toured with the national company of *The Wizard of Oz* for a number of years, with Mickey Rooney starring as the Wizard. My mother played the Wicked Witch of the West, a role for which she needed to learn to fly high above the stage on a broom, which was hilarious (as well as physically challenging) because she celebrated her seventy-first birthday on the road with that show. There were over one hundred people in the traveling company, plus a huge crew and sets. It played at Madison Square Garden, then traveled throughout the country.

In 2000, my mother appeared on Broadway in George C. Wolfe's production of Michael John LaChiusa's *The Wild Party,* with Mandy Patinkin and Toni Collette, which brought her her third Tony nomination, at age seventy-three (for Best Performance by a Featured Actress in a Musical, ultimately won by Karen Ziemba for "Contact"). She followed this up by touring throughout the U.S., as an uncharacteristically sassy Fairy Godmother in Rodgers and Hammerstein's *Cinderella,* a spectacular show that was staged again, three years later, at the New York City Opera. This second production was particularly poignant for my mother, as she had always said that if she hadn't become *Eartha Kitt,* then she would have wanted most to be an opera singer. (Marion Anderson and Leontyne Price were two renowned opera singers whom she greatly admired.) So to perform at the New York City Opera at Lincoln Center was a dream come true for her.

From 1991 until her death in 2008, I remained my mother's only manager, and she my only client. This was not a career I had chosen to pursue. I had never had any interest in becoming an entertainment manager or talent agent. Not at all. What started out as just a good idea at the time—going to work for my mother— evolved into a wonderful "life path."

It not only allowed me to work while simultaneously tending to both generations that I was flanked by, but also served an even more important purpose. It was a synergy, a partnership, a deeper connection with the woman who had given me life. A dependance, I guess you could say. On each other. As a baby and young child, my mother had been my protector. As an adult, I was hers.

When I talk about my life with my mother, people often say, "You had such an amazing connection and an amazing love." Yes, that's true. But I don't want people to think that this was all Nirvana. There were conflicts—internal conflicts, maybe—but very real ones, nonetheless. We were still, always, mother and daughter.

I really do believe that I was the perfect fit for her. Because even though I may have thought I wanted to pursue a different direction, or at least to have had other options, I know that the choices I ultimately made were the right ones. I don't feel that I ever missed out, or lacked something. I look back on my life as a whole, and I think the path I chose was right.

That may mean that I sacrificed myself somewhat for my mother. But I feel that was the right thing to do. For both of us. I think that I did it for myself as much as I did it for her.

After all, I was blessed with such richness, and so much love and appreciation. And humor. We both benefited. I certainly didn't lose out at all. And because we worked together, it was often about "us." My mother liked it that she was the front man onstage and I was the front man offstage. We made a good team.

I posted a picture of the two of us on Facebook one Mother's Day, and someone commented, "I'm so jealous!" I understand why. I mean, I was this wonderful woman's whole world! And I was even more blessed to have understood that while she was alive.

I know that, in many ways, my mother was the priority in my life. For my generation, it tends to be the other way around more. The priority is usually placed on the kids. I was lucky enough to have it both ways.

I was able to be there for my mother whenever she needed me. At the same time, my mother gave me the ability to have a life with my children, even though I had to do some juggling to make sure that she always felt important, too. Sometimes my kids would accompany us on the road. But there were also times I would have to say to her, "Your grandson needs me. I need to go to his hockey game. That's where I'll be this weekend."

I had the best of both worlds.

I was able to have this experience and still be there for my own family. Just as my mother had been there for me. She was lucky, too—lucky to be able to take me to work with her.

Yes, she worked hard to get that luck. But we both reaped the benefits of that. Most people can't take their kids to work with them.

And most people can't be with their mothers all of the time . . . especially as their mothers get older and, eventually, get sick.

CHAPTER 36

Curtain Call

Every day is a gift. Every day is a blessing.

My mother never missed a performance—ever. Even if she was sick. But in 2008, she wasn't just sick. She was dying. Although we didn't know it at the time, her last performance ever would be late that September, with the Virginia Symphony.

She had cancer.

And not just cancer. Stage 3 colon cancer. That was the diagnosis. She was in terrible pain. Her makeup artist, Carlo, and her longtime music director, Daryl Waters, and I kept looking at her, and each other, and wondering, "How is she ever going to go out there like this and sing?"

She was in such intense pain that she could barely stand up. But the second she stepped out onto the stage and the spotlight hit her, it was as if the pain just vanished. She was able to perform for ninety straight minutes, belting it out as if she were fifty years old. You would never in a million years have guessed that she was actually eighty-one. Or critically ill. But after those ninety minutes, she came off the stage and practically collapsed.

Why did she push herself like that? Why would anyone in their right mind do it? The answer was simple. My mother's fans, to her, were family. They were the family she had never had. They gave her back an abundance of love and affection. The last thing she ever wanted to do was disappoint them. She was also not one to go back on her word. A commitment was a commitment. She always rose to the occasion.

That would be the last occasion to which she would ever rise, however, even with her indefatigable spirit. We soon realized that we would have to cancel all of her remaining engagements.

January was usually the month that my mother performed at the Café Carlyle in New York. She'd had a residency there for almost thirteen years. But by mid-December, I looked at her and shook my head. "Mom," I said, "I hate to break this to you, but I don't think you're making it to the Carlyle next month."

I had no choice. Any fantasy that either one of us had that she would recover from this illness had to be let go. She knew this as well as I did. But that was it. Once she came to terms with that reality, she deteriorated quickly. She became a frail old lady. Yes, she was eighty-one by now, but you wouldn't have known that a week earlier, or even the day before. Aside from the pain that her cancer caused, my mother had still had the attitude and energy of a woman half her age. It was when she realized that she would no longer go on—go onstage, that is, and continue being in front of her fans to do what she loved—that she became her actual age. She gave up the fight. All of a sudden, she really had nothing left to look forward to.

Yes, she still had me, and my family. But the thing that had motivated her and propelled her to keep going for most of her life had been being *Eartha Kitt.* Having to become this persona, the one that she had created for herself so long ago. Once that was taken away from her, she felt, "What purpose do I serve?"

She was still a mother, of course. Once a mother, always a mother, no matter how old your children may get. But I was grown, with a family of my own, and she knew I'd be OK. When you're a performer, though, your work is never done. Your fans expect you to be the person they have come to know and love. And that love and adulation is energizing and inspiring. Her fans expected her to be *the* Eartha Kitt. She loved it. She needed it. Needed to be Eartha Kitt.

But now she was Eartha Mae again. And Eartha Mae was very sick.

Up until that point, my mother had always been incredibly healthy. She had suffered from rheumatoid arthritis, but not until late in her life. Then, over the Christmas holidays in 2007, it suddenly got much worse.

The pain was so bad that she couldn't do almost anything with her hands. She couldn't write. She couldn't do her needlepoint. So we went to see a rheumatologist.

He gave her every blood test on the planet and said that they indicated her rheumatoid arthritis wasn't that terrible. But he thought there might be some type of internal bleeding. She needed to go see her internist as soon as possible.

The internist sent her for a colonoscopy and an endoscopy.

And that's when they found the cancer.

She was eighty then, and up to that point she had never once had a colonoscopy. My mother was part of a generation of people who didn't go to the doctor very often. It didn't help that her closest relative, her aunt Mamie in Harlem, had gotten sick with some kind of stomach ailment, gone into the hospital, and then suddenly died when my mother was only twenty-four. This didn't exactly enhance my mother's eagerness to seek medical attention herself as she got older.

Plus, she was a woman who was very hearty and thought of herself as uber fit. "I'm healthy!" she thought. "I don't need to go to the doctor." So she didn't go too often. She didn't get regular checkups, or go for diagnostic tests. Yes, she got bronchitis a lot. That was an issue she often grappled with as a singer. But when you go to the doctor for bronchitis, they treat the symptoms. They give you an antibiotic. They don't give you a colonoscopy.

Needless to say, I have since had four colonoscopies myself. It's essential for everyone to get these tests, starting at age fifty for the general population (or earlier if prescribed by your doctor). If my mother had gone for them herself, then her condition might have been detected much earlier.

But by the time they found her cancer, it had already metastasized. She began getting chemotherapy, but eight months later she was suddenly in excruciating pain.

My mother went into the hospital on November 24, 2008, two days before Thanksgiving. It was Jason's eighteenth birthday and two days before my forty-seventh.

I spent that day sitting in the hospital with Allan, waiting for my mother to have emergency surgery. She was in so much pain, and her stomach was so distended from the cancer, that they were hoping to give her some relief. But they weren't able to find a surgical team to come in and perform the surgery until late that night.

Sitting in the waiting room, desperately hoping for some shred of good news, I began to think. "Forty-seven years ago today, my mother was in the hospital giving me life. Now here I am in the hospital, hoping they can give her life back to *her*."

Moments later, the surgeon came in. "We opened her up, and I was afraid that if I touched anything in there, I would do too much damage," she said solemnly. "The cancer is everywhere. I'm unable to do anything more." They had to simply close her back up.

The doctor said she might have three months left, but even that was doubtful.

The next day was Thanksgiving, but no one in our family felt like celebrating, least of all me. I spent that day in the hospital. In fact, I was basically there with my mother from the Monday before Thanksgiving until we took her home in the middle of December. During that time, I only left her side to go home at ten o'clock each night, then would return at six or seven in the morning. A nurse would watch her overnight while I was gone.

One Sunday while she was in the hospital, a priest came into her room. It wasn't to administer last rites, or anything like that. He was just a fan. He wanted to see if she needed anything, whether it be company or a little comfort. But my mother showed no interest in conversing with him. She barely even said a word.

That, of course, left me the usual task of trying to fill in the conversation. "So, your Holiness," I began, doing my best to make chitchat. But in a short while, he left.

A few minutes later, we were watching television when my mother made a comment, totally out of the blue. "I don't understand why God does [such-and-such] . . ."

I looked at her and said, "You just had the man in the room who has a direct line to God, and you wait until he leaves to ask *me*? *I* can't answer that question!"

Then we laughed. We laughed until we almost cried. That's what the last few weeks of her life were like—filled with laughter and just spending time together.

We soon decided that she would be more comfortable in her own house, with hospice care. And so I took her home to Connecticut.

Once she was there, someone from hospice would come in every day. But she didn't want anyone staying with her overnight, so she would manage on her own.

For most people, this would have been a sad time. But that's not how we lived, Mom and me. We weren't going to lose our senses of humor now. I remember propping her up with pillows at one point and asking, perhaps a little too loudly, "Are you OK?"

And she looked at me and said, "I can hear you just fine. I'm dying. I'm not deaf!"

I remember saying to Allan one day, "She's having the time of her life! She has me 24/7. This is her greatest dream come true!"

I would only leave her house when necessary, to go get her something from the store. She clearly didn't have much time left. We all knew that. So every time I went to run an errand for her, I would say to her, "Please don't die while I'm gone! It would be really, really, really unpleasant if I came back and you were dead."

And she would give me a wry little smile and say, "I can't make any promises."

We'd brought a hospital bed into her room, and we would sit there together watching TV shows and old movies. My mother still loved her murder mysteries. From *Murder, She Wrote* and *Columbo* reruns to forensic shows on cable TV, she still wanted to try to solve the crime herself, and still wanted to know who'd done it.

One day, Carlo came over and put up a Christmas tree in her bedroom bedecked with colorful lights. The room overlooked a meadow, with a river running at the bottom. Outside, the snow was falling. It was a magical view.

My mother, Eartha, who was of the earth, had always loved Nature so much. Now she was getting the most beautiful glimpse of it.

We couldn't have managed, however, without the help of the amazing hospice nurses. What an incredible career path that is! I would talk to them while my mother was asleep. "Your patients don't ever get better," I said to one. "How hard is that? You're treating people and their families, and there's never going to be a happy ending."

There was no happy ending in store for us now, either. That, I knew. And I'm sure my mother did, too.

People would say to me afterward, "What did you do together during those last few weeks? Did you sit and have deep talks?"

No, we didn't. We didn't need to. My mother and I knew exactly how we felt about each other. She had spent a lifetime telling me how much she loved me. It was a blessing that I was always very aware of.

So we talked about other things. Things that we had done together. Places we had gone. People we had known. And things that we had seen.

Strangely enough, she had begun seeing new things now. Things that I couldn't see myself because, I promise you, they weren't there. She kept seeing people. People that she couldn't identify. "Don't you see that little girl standing there?" she would ask.

Nope. No girl. Little or otherwise. I was the only other person in the room.

The hospice nurse told me that she often heard this from her patients. Then she qualified that.

"You don't know if these visions are spirits or imaginary," she said, "but the patients believe they are real." No one could really say what they were. My mother was now on morphine. Could it be the morphine that was inducing these mysterious visions?

One day in late December, my mother wanted to take a bath. Her skin had gotten so dry that every inch of her body itched. She'd been in the hospital or in bed for weeks now. She wanted to take a bath with bath oil and enjoy soaking in a nice, warm tub.

So I drew her a bath and helped her climb in. My mother had a gorgeous bathroom filled with stone and marble. It had a large, deep soaking tub, and she was so happy lying there in the satiny water.

When the bath was over, she wanted to get out. But she couldn't get out of the bathtub because she didn't have a lot of strength anymore. She was really weak. And her bathtub was really deep.

"You have to help me get out of the tub," she told me. "I can't do it myself."

So I tried to help her. Tried my best. But she kept slipping right through my hands. She was coated with oil.

She had grown so tiny and frail by now that I could have lifted her if she were dry. But she wasn't dry. She was as slick and slippery as a wet seal.

It was my worst nightmare, but the two of us soon became hysterical. I was laughing so hard that I almost peed in my pants. It got to the point at which I couldn't get her out of the bath mostly because I was laughing so hard. Every time I would lift her up, she would slip from my hands again and slide back down into the tub.

"You have to be stronger!" she ordered me. "Please! Get me out!"

"I can't," I insisted. "I'm doing the best I can, but you're like dead weight."

"I'm not dead yet!" she replied indignantly. And then we would laugh again.

"Don't you make me call the fire department," I told her. "If they have to come over here and get you out of this bathtub, we will both be embarrassed."

It was like a Monty Python movie. That's how funny it was. I finally got into the tub with her, and she put her foot on my leg. But she still kept slipping from my grasp.

I don't know how I did it, but I finally did pull her out and got her back into bed. The two of us ended up exhausted, oily, and laughing so hard that we both cried.

This, as I said, should have been a time of tremendous sadness. But we were still finding reasons to laugh. For, as she had said, she wasn't dead yet. I am so blessed that these times are also part of all the memories I have of the life I shared with my mother.

There we were, Eartha and Kitt, giggling together, ever connected throughout our lives, even now, when it was something so awful. It was clear that she didn't have many more days left. Yet we were still both able to find the humor in life.

And, yes, even in death.

That's how my mother lived. "Don't take anything too seriously," she would say. You can't take *anything* in life too seriously. But most of all, don't take yourself too seriously."

There are so many times in our lives when we find ourselves looking at the dark side. My mother felt that we worry too much about so many things. If we would just lighten up a bit, it wouldn't necessarily change the situation, she believed, but it would make life much more pleasant.

Being able to find laughter in almost every moment was truly a gift with which my mother blessed me. And that we were able to laugh together, even during those last few days, made for wonderful memories, even in such extraordinarily difficult moments. These were among the greatest gifts of all.

By now, she wasn't coming out with as many "Kittisms" or pearls of wisdom anymore, but she still had a lot to say. And she still had some final thoughts that she wanted to express. So we got her some recording equipment into which she would be able to speak.

We set the device up in her bedroom a few days before Christmas. Yet by now she barely had the energy or capacity to say a word. So we weren't able to record any of her remaining thoughts or observations.

The hospice nurse told me what I could expect when the end was near. "She's going to just fade away," she said. "At some point, she'll begin to lose her speech. Then she'll stop eating, and she'll stop drinking, and then it will just sort of happen."

She made it sound like it would be very peaceful. But boy, was it anything but!

On Christmas Day, my mother and I were watching TV alone. Everyone else had taken the day off in order to be with their families.

My husband was home with the kids, three miles away. But then my mother began acting strange. So a little before 2 P.M., I called my house. One of our daughters picked up.

"Please tell Dad that I need some help," I said to her firmly. "Tell him to please come over here right now."

I don't know why I suddenly felt this need to call him. I didn't actually think my mother was dying at that moment. I just thought she was very ill, and that I needed an extra set of hands.

I did need those extra hands. For the moment that Allan arrived, things changed almost instantly.

By now, my mother had lost her speech entirely. She had stopped speaking about two days earlier. But she had still remained alert. Her eyes were wide open. I could tell if she was hungry, or if she wanted water. And she could still comprehend me and make her needs known.

She could also still make herself heard. And that's what she was doing right now, loud and clear. She literally left this earth screaming at the top of her lungs.

Tears were streaming down her face. And she was screaming with this sort of—this primal, animal-like sound. It was intense!

That's when I realized that she was actually going. Going *now*. But not willingly. And not quietly, for sure.

In typical mother-daughter fashion, I soon began screaming right back at her. "You can go!" I cried, my lips close to her ear, holding her to me with all my might.

"You can go!" I kept yelling again and again as I wept. "I'll be all right! I'll be all right!" Because it suddenly became clear to me that she had been waiting. Waiting until I wasn't alone. Now that Allan was there with me, she could die. I wasn't going to be alone.

It was an incredibly emotional moment, with these fierce, guttural sounds coming out of my mother as she screamed at the top of her lungs. Then, all of a sudden, she fell silent. And I knew that she was gone.

Gone.

Silence. Complete silence. From all three of us.

"Is she . . . dead?" I sobbed to Allan.

"I don't know," he said, equally stunned. We both looked at each other, bewildered. We didn't know what to do next. That's when I said, "Well, whoever is at those pearly gates waiting for her, they are going to get quite a handful. Because she is not coming peacefully, that's for sure!"

Maybe I was in shock. Maybe it was disbelief. Or maybe I was able to joke, even at that moment, because as I said, my mother had taught me to find the humor in everything.

I sat holding her hand, not wanting to let go, while Allan called the hospice nurse and Jaki. When the nurse arrived, she asked if I wanted to help wipe my mother's face and clean her up before the people from the funeral parlor arrived. I was standing in the bathroom with a washcloth, waiting for the water in the faucet to get warm, when she came in, touched my arm, and said gently, "I don't think she's going to care if the water is hot or cold, dear."

"You don't know my mother," I replied. "Dead or not, if I put a cold washcloth to her face, she's going to come back and be mad at both of us!" I still felt that I needed to take care of her. That's what I had been born to do.

Death is so final. One second she had been there, screaming, and then, in an instant, she was gone. There was this body lying there, but there was no longer a person occupying it.

It's almost impossible to comprehend. The brain has a really hard time processing the idea that someone you deeply loved just went "poof" and then disappeared into midair, as though they had evaporated.

Everything had changed. Everything was suddenly different. Our lives had been so intertwined. Not only because we were mother and daughter, but because we also worked together so closely and lived only three miles away from each other. We had seen each other or spoken almost daily.

But now there was no more Eartha on this earth. In the days and weeks that followed, I remember thinking how I really understood why religion is so important to people. How, in times of death and despair, so many feel the need to cling to their faith.

I would often stand outside, look up at the sky, and realize why Heaven is so real for so many people. Your emotions want to believe that your loved one is somewhere. That they've gone someplace. Maybe they're not still in their body, but they are still who they were. Otherwise it just doesn't make sense. Logically, it doesn't compute. I would look up at the sky and ask, "Where are you? Are you somewhere? Are you everywhere? Where did you go?"

I don't know where she went, but I can tell you where I took her. My mother had always said that she wanted to be cremated after she died. "Don't let me take up any excess space when I'm gone," she would say to me. "It's a waste."

How could I not honor that wish?

After I picked her ashes up, I called Allan, crying hysterically. My mother was now in millions of little pieces, so that you couldn't ever put her back together again. Obviously, you could never have put her back together again anyway. But logic wasn't quite within my grasp.

There's this feeling that you want to believe that, somehow, the person you have lost is going to make it back to you. That you are going to be able to see him or her again someday. But if you have taken away their body, how can that come true?

And what if my mother wanted her body back?

I realized that question made no logical sense, either. But at that moment, I had just taken away any possibility of my mother ever coming back to me, or certainly coming back in that body.

I was later telling the story of her passing, and someone said, "I can't believe you're talking about the moment of death!" But to me, it was such a powerful moment. It was another experience my mother and I had together. It was one more piece of her sharing who she was, and of teaching me. Everything she does—or *did*— was a lesson.

CHAPTER 37

Ashes to Ashes

I am learning all the time.
The tombstone will be my diploma.

My mother had wanted her ashes to be spread into Nature after she was gone. As Eartha, she had always been "of the earth." Now she would be part of it again.

But selfishly, perhaps, I have never been able to give her back to the earth. I just haven't been ready to part with any part of her. I did get her a nice birdbath, though, because she was obsessed with birds. My mother loved to watch the birds outside her window, and would often sit with books, learning about the different species she saw. Birds' behavior patterns had always fascinated her, and she kept bird feeders and birdbaths around her property to keep them coming back.

The birdbath that I found is a very special one, however. Its base is constructed to hold an urn. And I had a plaque mounted on it bearing the dates of her birth and death, as well as the words "Here's to Life," the name of the song my mother closed her shows with for decades. I have yet to place her in there, though. It's too cold outside in the wintertime here, and I worry that she's going to be cold. (Don't try to find any logic in that statement.)

I asked the funeral parlor to separate out some of her ashes before they gave them to me because, for years, my mother and I had joked about something. We talked about having her made into a diamond when she was gone. Seriously! I had found a company that takes the ashes of your loved one and uses the carbon to make a diamond. It had been a running joke between us, long before she even got sick.

My mother and I, as I've said before, were different in many ways. My mother did not love jewelry. She felt that jewelry was a burden. Something to worry about losing or having stolen. That's why she loved the earth. Soil. Land. "Don't me give jewelry," she would say, "give me land. Because they're not making any more of it." I, on the other hand, have rarely seen a piece of jewelry I didn't like.

So whenever my mother would make fun of me and say, "What are you going to do with me after I'm dead?" I would tease her by replying, "I'm going to make you into a huge diamond for all eternity. And wear you prominently around my neck."

I came to find out, though, that the diamonds made from the ashes are teeny. They're just a little speck. You can barely even see them.

"I'm not going to make her into just this little speck," I thought. "She deserves much more than that." So I haven't had my mother turned into a diamond just yet.

But I have kept that small, separate portion of her ashes inside a little ceramic heart. It sits on my desk, which is actually my mother's old desk, the one at which she wrote her three autobiographies, and book on fitness and health. All in longhand, I might add. The color of the desk has faded through the years, but my mother's hands and her spirit remain ingrained in this piece of furniture, which I am now using to discover my own voice. It seems only fitting that that heart-shaped box with her ashes should sit next to me there.

In 2016, the governor of South Carolina signed a proclamation declaring January 17th to be Eartha Kitt Day. And when it was first observed, in 2017, Allan and I went down for the occasion, and I brought that ceramic heart with me.

My mother's hometown wanted to hold its own special celebration in her honor. Even though my mother had had a very tough time growing up there, she had always remembered where she came from. She had been born in this small town called North, South Carolina. I decided it was important to come full-circle and bring her back to that place.

So, together with representatives from the town of North, we decided to hold a gala in the North Middle/High School Gym to celebrate the day. The mayor at the time, Patty Carson, had mentioned a local organization called the Cooperative Ministries of North. It's a group of thirteen churches from neighboring towns that all work together to help their members and neighbors who may be in need, whether it be with food, medicine, diapers, clothing, a ride to a doctor, or that someone has a roof that needs repairing. So, as part of the celebration, we held an auction of some of my mother's personal items that I brought down with me, and the proceeds went to benefit the Cooperative Ministries.

About three hundred people turned out for it. North only has about seven hundred residents, so having three hundred come to this dinner was pretty special. It was important to me that the event be a fundraiser because I wanted to give something back to the town. And I wanted to share some of my mother with them.

Almost everyone I spoke with that evening had a similar story to tell. They all went something like this: "My mother said that my grandmother is your mother's cousin." Or, "My grandmother had the same history." Or, "My aunt would tell me stories about your mother as a child."

It was so uplifting to see the love that they all had for my mother, and the pride they exhibited about her having been born there. Only a handful of those in attendance had ever met her, though. One was a ninety-year-old gentleman, who rode his bike to the gala that evening. A woman who was also in her nineties remembered her, too. She got very emotional when she said to me, "They really didn't do well by your mother down here. She was really badly treated by the family that took her in. Those kids were just horrible to her."

It was interesting to hear that. This woman had lived a really long life and was barely able to walk on her own anymore, and yet remembering how terribly they had treated my mother still really choked her up.

It's funny, isn't it? So many times, you listen to your parents telling old stories, and you roll your eyes and think, "Oh, boy, here we go again! How are they going to exaggerate this one today?" But when I got to hear people from her hometown talk, they only corroborated what my mother had said and how difficult life had been for her.

I began to wonder if I had made a terrible mistake in bringing that heart containing some of her ashes down with me.

Or had I?

There was the Baptist church that my mother had sung in when she was a little girl. And after Allan and I left the Eartha Kitt Day event, at around eleven that night, I said him, "I want to go put a little bit of my mother into the ground by that church."

Yes, I remained a little conflicted about this. My mother hadn't had a great experience growing up down there. *Should* I bury some of her there? I wasn't sure that she wanted to be there. Then again, wouldn't that really be coming full circle?

After all, Eartha was her given name. She had been genuinely "of the earth." And she had always said that she was "just a poor cotton picker from the South." So the two of us began driving down a two-lane highway toward this little Baptist church.

We headed down a very dark, deserted road in search of a church I had only glimpsed in an old black-and-white photo. Then I saw it, a secluded building, lit up by floodlights, and we pulled into a gravel-covered parking area.

It was about 11:30 by now and pitch dark everywhere, except for the front of the church. Allan followed behind me as I started walking into the tiny adjacent cemetery.

I wandered all around this cemetery, in total darkness, using the narrow beam from the flashlight on my cellphone to see as best as I could, trying to find the perfect spot in which to bury some of my mother's ashes.

You know what it's like when dogs go to the bathroom outside, and they just keep walking around looking for the exact right spot? It feels like an eternity. After a while, you say, "Just go already! Go anywhere!" Well, that was me in that cemetery.

I'm walking here. I'm walking there. Allan says to me, "She'll be fine no matter where you put her."

"I can't just put her anywhere," I fire back. "I have to find the right spot for her!"

I keep going deeper and deeper in, closer to the forest that's behind the church. By now, I have literally spent twenty minutes trying to find the perfect spot for my mother. But I realize that

Allan is right. So I get down on the ground and push back a little bit of dirt with my fingernails. Then I dig a teeny hole, open the little bag inside the ceramic heart, and pour out some of her ashes. Just a tiny bit, though. Barely a teaspoonful.

Then I cover them back up.

Allan is standing there watching me. "That's it?" he asks incredulously. "That's all you're putting here? That wasn't even a toe!"

But now I have tears streaming down my face. "I can't put *all* of her here," I cry. "I don't know if she even wants to *be* here."

He shakes his head. "She won't be able to walk around, you know," he jokes, trying to make me smile. "You didn't give her enough ashes to be able to take a stroll around the place. That was barely a toenail's worth."

That wasn't true. It was at least a toenail's worth. But at that point, that was all I was prepared to part with. I still wasn't sure that I was doing the right thing. Doing what she would have wanted. But it was late. And it was done.

So we got back into the car and drove away.

The South was emotionally conflicting for my mother. Those cotton fields were filled with pain. Yet, to her dying day, she'd identified herself as being from the South. I, too, was feeling conflicted on her behalf. And still felt the need to protect her.

Selfishly, I guess, I still wanted to keep her almost all to myself. So in the end, I gave the South just a tiny taste.

I gave that earth only a little bit of Eartha.

I have always thought the rituals that different religions and societies have created surrounding the end of life are fascinating. But now I more fully appreciate and understand how important they are.

When my mother died, thinking back on all the experiences in my life—and the different cultures and religions that she exposed me to—really made me understand the importance of cemeteries, graves, churches, temples, or whatever it is that you believe. Whether you build a mausoleum, or you're an Egyptian pharaoh having pyramids erected, there are so many rituals that revolve around death and what the people who are left behind do for the dead; so many things we do to keep the memories alive.

I still have all of my mother's recordings and films. I have a treasure trove of her letters, journals, scrapbooks, costumes, and other memorabilia. I still have all of her *stuff.* But I want to believe that she herself is still somewhere, and that she is still connected somehow.

My mother had so many friends and other people she knew who died before her—old friends like James Dean, Orson Welles, Paul Newman, Nat King Cole, and Marilyn Monroe. There were so many people she missed and wished that she could talk to again. So I think she must be very busy. She has a lot of people to catch up with. Maybe now's her opportunity.

She may be out looking for her own mother. Maybe she has even finally found her father.

But I would like to think that she is still, in some form, somewhere in this world. And so, because my mother loved birds so much, every time I see a bird, I say, "Yup, there's my mother!"

My husband, who has heard this a few too many times, rolls his eyes and says, "Every bird cannot be your mother."

"Oh, yes it can," I shoot back. "You don't know my mother!"

My mother was a true believer in spirits. She often referred to talking to spirits and seeing them in old places.

She also believed in some type of afterlife. I don't think she believed in reincarnation, though, as much as she believed that your spirit goes on. The body dies. The body gives out. But the spirit carries on.

When Carrie Fisher died, and then Debbie Reynolds passed away the very next day, I remember saying, "That would have been my mother." My mother often said to me as a little girl, "If anything ever happens to you, they're going to have to take me, too. If anything happened to you, I would just go."

Debbie Reynolds' son said in an interview, "My mother died from a broken heart. She couldn't exist without Carrie."

And I thought, "My mother was exactly the same way with me."

I guess the feeling was mutual, though. It's been hard for me not having her.

As a young adult, I used to think that when it was time for my mother to pass, she would say, "My part is done in this world. I'm ready," and then she would walk peacefully into the sunset, close her eyes, and just go. But the reality was far from that. She didn't leave this world that way at all. She left it kicking and screaming.

I think that was her survival instinct speaking, even after she had lost all words. That's who she was.

A survivor.

I honestly believe that, on some level, you are either genetically predisposed to be a survivor, or you're not. There are people who just survive. My mother was a survivor, for sure.

When I watched her leave this earth and transition to the next place, wherever that may be, I realized that it was that survival instinct in her that wasn't going to let go easily. She wasn't going to give up without a fight.

So she did not "go gentle into that good night," as the Dylan Thomas poem says. She was a force to be reckoned with in life. And I don't know what she's like in the afterlife, but I know she was certainly a force to be reckoned with on her way there.

I had known that she wouldn't be here forever, but I'd always imagined that she would be around until well into her nineties, you know? And so, at times, I wonder.

From long before I was born, she was this larger-than-life sex symbol. At eighty years old, my mother was still standing on the stage looking like she was twenty years younger. She looked gorgeous and amazing! I don't know how she would have felt about herself, or what it would have been like for her to look in the mirror, at, say, ninety.

My mother got spared from ever getting old. Up until the end, she was still Eartha Kitt. She was still full of life, glamorous and young at heart. And I think that was a gift. The alternative might have been so much harder for her. It would have been tough for me, too. It was hard for me to see her age so quickly, as she did those last few weeks.

In the end, she was little more than a skeleton. She was probably down to eighty pounds. At her heaviest, she had only been about 118. But she was still far from her usual self. She looked gaunt and emaciated.

In the entertainment business, people expect you to not age visibly at all. Yet my mother never tried to hold on to youth, as much as she tried to always look her best. She always remained active, and even at eighty was still dancing up a storm, exercising daily, and stretching. She was always incredibly limber. You could see that when she was onstage.

She was also proud of her gray hairs, although she didn't have a lot of them. People didn't see whatever gray she had because she usually wore wigs when she performed. But she loved the gray hair that she had! There were times when she got her hair dyed that she would ask them to leave in some of the gray. She had a little patch of it right in front.

"I've worked very hard to get this gray," she would explain proudly.

She loved her gray. Loved her wrinkles, too. Loved how her face had matured. To her, these were all medals of honor.

"This is my badge of survival," she would say. "I've made it through! I'm still here!"

That may be why she gave that name to one of her many books—*I'm Still Here.* It was also the name of a Stephen Sondheim song from *Follies* that she often sang.

Good times and bum times
I've seen them all and, my dear
I'm still here.

Life to her was a badge of honor. "I haven't done anything to cover up or hide," she would say. "I don't have anything to hide *from*."

She was very proud of her life, and of who she was. She would not have done anything any differently.

I find that so incredible. I mean, my mother was not flawless, by any means. But I remember her declaring near the end, "I've lived an amazing life!" It was something that she always said, for as long as I can remember. And whether or not she realized she only had a few weeks left, she said that again when it was coming to an end.

"I've lived an amazing life!" she said. "I've exceeded all expectations—my own and everyone else's. I have no regrets. I wouldn't do anything differently."

Knowing that she actually meant that, I looked at her and thought to myself, "What an amazing way to feel!"

She owned all of her behavior. It was, "This is who I am. This is *what* I am. Take me as I am!"

She closed all of her concerts with the song "Here's to Life," by Artie Butler and Phyllis Molinary, because the lyrics captured so well who she was. They spoke to every part of her essence.

No complaints and no regrets
I still believe in chasing dreams and placing bets
And I have learned that all you give is all you get
So give it all you've got . . .

That was truly my mother. She did give it all that she had, and with her, it was, "Take me warts and all." She made no excuses for herself.

Epilogue

God may not be there when you want Him,
but He is always on time.

The first year after my mother died was particularly difficult for me because our lives were totally intertwined. We lived close to each other. We traveled together. We worked together all the time. I was her only family, and other than my husband and children, she was mine.

The first Mother's Day after she died was especially challenging. Allan and my kids could tell that I wasn't up for any kind of activity. "Mom just wants to be by herself," they realized. If I couldn't be with my mother, then I just wanted to do nothing.

They were around me, in the house, but I was in no mood to go out to lunch or dinner. Which was sort of how I felt throughout the first two years after my mother died.

That meant that the following Mother's Day was just as difficult. The day no longer held the same meaning to me, even though I was still a mother myself. I would never again be the one giving the Mother's Day cards. It was surreal. I remember going into the living room, where my mother's ashes were, and saying to her right out loud, "Happy Mother's Day."

"I can't believe I'll never hear you talk to me again!" I added. That concept was hard to grasp.

Yes, I could still watch one of her movies, or listen to her music, but I was never going to actually see her look at me and speak to me again. I couldn't comprehend that.

It was a beautiful day outside, but I just sat inside, trying to find something on television that wouldn't trigger a deluge from my tear ducts. I was flipping through the channels when I suddenly came upon a movie that looked vaguely familiar.

The "info" button told me the title was *Anything but Love*. This was a 2002 romantic musical comedy written by and starring actress Isabel Rose, in which my mother had made a cameo appearance, playing herself. I had only seen it once, when we went to the premiere, but I had been present during filming and recognized the set. In this movie, a young woman who longs to be a singer goes to my mother seeking advice. I wasn't sure at what point in the story my mother appeared, or if I had already missed her. I didn't care. I was riveted. Waiting. Hoping. For what, I didn't know.

Then, as I am sitting there watching, the scene comes on in which the lead character approaches a door on which an oversized star sparkles above my mother's name. The young woman's hand is shaking as she gets up the courage to knock outside her idol's dressing room, and then an unmistakable voice responds, "Yes?"

My mother opens the door, and now the point of view of the camera is strictly angled from the young woman's perspective. As the camera slowly pans from my mother's satin shoes up the slinky, silk jersey gown, it ends with a full frontal shot of her looking directly into the lens and giving this girl the sage advice she was searching for.

It was as though she was speaking to me directly. I'm not sure if the young woman in the film got the answer she needed, but I know that I received the message loud and clear. The tears streamed down my face as I was able to see my mother looking right at me, one more time.

This was so intense that I wrote a poem about it.

MOTHER'S DAY 2010

Guess you were listening after all
I asked for you and you answered my call.
I heard your voice and then saw your face
Not far away from where I keep your space.
You looked so good, your voice sounded so strong
It's hard to believe you've been gone for so long.

I sat watching you there, up on the screen
My eyes filled with tears as you went through the scene.
Your presence was so real that it made me upset
I just wanted to grab onto that big TV set.
Oh, how I miss you, even more every day
With each step I feel fear as I make my own way.
Mom, I must thank you for hearing my plea
Knowing how much seeing you there meant to me.
Feeling you with me gives me reason to say
That today was a truly memorable Mother's Day.

I don't know what you believe. But to me, somebody somewhere had clearly heard something. Because for that scene in that movie to come on, right on that day, after I had made that statement out loud? Well, stranger things have happened, I suppose. But was this really just pure chance, just a coincidence? Is *anything?*

My mother died on December 25, 2008. Christmas Day. Ever since then, it has become a tradition for my family to go away together, just the six of us, each Christmas. We rent a house somewhere and just spend quiet time together.

The irony is not lost on me that my mother died on Christmas Day, when "Santa Baby," the song written for her in 1953 by Phil Springer and Joan Javits, is being played throughout the world. I guess she really wanted to make sure she left her mark, and she would never be forgotten.

And to this day, she remains one of the reigning queens of Christmas music.

But for those first few years, during the holiday season, standing in the middle of Bed, Bath & Beyond, Starbucks, or Barnes & Noble, and suddenly hearing my mother's voice? That was not easy.

Now whenever I hear it, I smile instead and say, "Thank you, Mom!"

Thank you for being my mother.

Thank you for being the unique, original, and extraordinary woman that you were.

Thank you for becoming—no, for *making* yourself—so much more than "just a poor cotton picker from the South."

Thank you, Mom, for being you, and for teaching me to be me.

Acknowledgments
Kitt Shapiro

Allan Rothschild, this project overwhelmed me in ways I never expected. You talked me off the ledge, wiped my tears, and prodded me along when I thought I would quit. Your guidance, support, and understanding of the importance of this book mean the world to me. I don't know how I would have made it through without you. Thank you.

Pattie Weiss Levy, you didn't flinch when taking on this project and the daunting task of unraveling my stories and organizing my thoughts. I am forever grateful for your perseverance and conviction in this project. Thank you for believing in this book from the second we met.

Jessica Case, thank you for seeing the beauty, importance, and impact of this relationship. And for your help guiding this book to its completion.

Russell Galen, you championed this love story between a mother and a daughter from day one. Thank you for your wisdom and sense of calm, when I was not.

Andrew Freedman, I am so happy you continue to take this ride with me. I know my mother and Patty Freedman are smiling and conspiring, wherever they are. Rachel Shapiro, you were born an "old soul" and are wise beyond your years. Thank you for reminding me that my "Don't Panic" tattoo is there for a reason. Your presence brings a smile to my face every day. I know Nana is beaming with pride. You make my heart sing.

Jason Shapiro, thank you for always showing me the importance of being passionate about what you do. Thank you for seeking me out when I was holed up in my room, exhausted and bleary-eyed, and checking in on me. I see so much of your grandmother in you. I am proud to be your mother.

Nicole Rothschild, thank you for your love, encouragement, and for listening. And for teaching me how to play Rummikub, so I could finally live out my dream of a family game night.

Eric Rothschild, thank you for being a perfect example of how caring is better said through actions than words.

Maki, your unconditional love and devotion comfort me like still having a little piece of my mother.

Carlo Geraci, there are no words for the years of love and laughter we were blessed to have shared.

Jaki Harris, you left us too soon. Guess my mother really needed you more.

Melissa Gladstone, Linda Revelli, Sheryl Udell, and Pam LaRocca: Team WEST. Thank you for your loyalty and laughter! You ladies make coming to work every day a joy.

Joan Korenchuk, thank you for your support, kindness, and composure.

Julie and Jim Migliaccio, I love you both. Debbie and Eli Hazan, with you around, life is never boring. Diane Karmen and Ronny Carroll, you help make my world more beautiful.

Dara Rothschild, thank you for always having my back. You rock!

Hugs to all my in-laws—Alan, Isabel, Addison, Stanley, Rita, Hillary, Rick, Dylan, and Jake.

Clara-Lisa Kabbaz, we have been sisters/best friends since we were little, and you continue to remind me that no matter how old we get, we are always young at heart. Jackie Nesbit and Jody Stern, love our memories.

Charles and Cari Shapiro, thanks for helping make our crazy family dynamic work.

Daryl Waters, you know how important you were to my mother. She loved you like a son. Thank you for always being there for her.

Phil Sandhaus and Lenore Kletter, thank you for the many years of hard work and devotion.

There are so many who have touched my life, and my mother's life, that I cannot name them all. You know who you are and what you meant to us. For that, I say thank you.

And to my mother's fans, old and new, thank you for helping me continue her legacy, because *Blessings Are Meant to Be Shared.*

Acknowledgments
Patricia Weiss Levy

You know the old story. It's universal, right? There are so many books, movies, plays, and even fairy tales about people who long to escape their ordinary existences to find adventure and see the world. Take Disney's *Beauty and the Beast.* Belle, its beautiful but homebound heroine, reads voraciously in search of vicarious thrills as she croons, "There must be more than this provincial life!"

Well, that, more or less, was my own story growing up (despite how chaotic coming of age in my family could be). But it clearly wasn't Kitt Shapiro's. I would like to thank Kitt for entrusting me to help tell her remarkable story, and for giving me all of the time that this took.

Many thanks also to our literary agent, Russell Galen, for introducing us to each other and making the literary "*shiddoch*" that gave birth to this book.

That birth would never have happened without our extraordinary editor, Jessica Case of Pegasus Books. Between the emails and updates she sent almost daily, from early in the morning to late at night, I'm not quite sure when she ever slept. She has my infinite gratitude for her patience, enthusiasm, expertise, and most of all for embracing this book and bringing it to life.

Unlike Kitt's multitalented mother, who lived and died with no regrets, I have at least one regret myself: Although I always knew *of* the iconic and incandescent Eartha Kitt, I never got to know her, meet her, or see her perform live. But in helping to craft these pages, I feel as if I got to know her, well beyond the sound of her unforgettable voice, and I hope all who read this do, too.

From the moment Kitt and I first met, I was struck by the many parallels in our lives, which go beyond our living in the same small state. She is the daughter of a jazz singer and performer; I have a daughter who is one, as well as a son who writes about jazz. Our mothers were born only a year apart, and died within a few months of each other at the age of 81. And although mine may never have attained world renown, she had her own troubled life that she managed to resiliently and resoundingly rise above.

More significantly, perhaps, I know what it is like to be loved fiercely and maybe even a bit too much by an adoring mother – Bunnie, who also made me her constant companion and confidante, and, at times, her whole world. Or is that a universal story, too?

There are many others in my own world to whom gratitude is due. So many friends buoyed me up and bore with me when I was too busy with this book to talk or even text: Ilisa Keith, Hallie Weiss, Liz Roth, Lois and Rafi Wurzel, Sally Wister, Dial Parrott, Pat Kazakoff, Stacey Savin, Catherine Fellows Johnson, Sari Agatston, Doreen Frankel, Jake Hurwitz, Paul and Kathy Wade, Anne Kan, Arlene Blum, Nada Kelly, Suzy Glantz, and Suzanne Eagle, as well as my brother and sister-in-law, Joel and Karen Weiss, and my cousin Susan Weiss.

In a year that rarely caught me out and about without a mask, I also cannot mask my appreciation to the many members of my women's book group, the Shayna Maidels, for their enduring friendship and moral support.

Most of all, though, there is my family. Infinite thanks go to my wise and witty son, Aidan Levy—without whom this book would never have seen the light of day, let alone be listed on Amazon—as well as his beautiful and brilliant wife, Kaitlin Mondello, an ever-calming presence who is goodness itself.

As the classic song on her "Looking at the Moon" album goes, "Got no checkbooks, got no banks, still I'd like to express my thanks . . ." to my talented, encouraging, kind, and caring daughter, Allegra Levy (who is my own confidante and constant companion). Boundless appreciation also to her invariably upbeat husband JP Sistenich, who never failed to crack me up when I was about to crumble.

Much love to my little granddaughter Diana, whose Dabda (as she has dubbed me) has been too busy lately to deliver soup, carrots, meatballs, or "more paint!" And to my next, soon-to-be-born baby grandchild . . . the light at the end of this endless tunnel.

And last of all, but surely not least, to my husband, Harlan James Levy, who put up with more than anyone's share of meltdowns, miserable moods, a chronically messy house, and dinners served unbelievably late, or sometimes not at all. Yes, there may be more than this provincial life . . . but why would I want it when I have our kids and you?